GLOBAL TRADING

GLOBAL TRADING

EDITED BY
MADS ANDENAS

BIICL
BRITISH INSTITUTE OF
INTERNATIONAL AND
COMPARATIVE LAW

Published and Distributed by
The British Institute of International and Comparative Law
Charles Clore House, 17 Russell Square, London WC1B 5JP

British Library Cataloguing in Publication Data
A Catalogue record of this book is available from the British Library

ISBN 0–903067–47–1

Typeset by Cambrian Typesetters
Frimley, Surrey
Printed in Great Britain by Biddles Ltd,
Guildford and King's Lynn

PREFACE

This document represents a Report of the British Institute on Global Trading and has been published as part of our Occasional Papers Series. The Report was discussed at a seminar at the British Institute in April 2002 under the title 'Global Agreements Between Manufacturers and Retailers'. Sir Jeremy Lever, KCMG, QC, was in the chair and speakers included Michael Hutchings, Frances Graupner and Dr Richard Bell. Different members of staff at the Institute have contributed to the Report, as have the members of a Steering Committee, to whom the Institute is very grateful. Comments are invited and should be addressed to the British Institute, either by post or by email to *info@biicl.org*.

The Report is set in the context of the changing manufacturer–retailer relationship, which has evolved as a consequence of developments in retailing and their influence on the market for consumer goods. This restructuring of market dynamics along with the increasing globalisation of business transactions poses a challenge to the traditional legal analysis of manufacturer–retailer relationships.

The trend towards retailer internationalisation has put pressure on suppliers to negotiate with retailers at the international level rather than solely at individual national levels. As retailers' interests become more global and they demand that their operations adopt a global focus, there will be an increasing demand for global supply contracts.

This Report is focused on one feature of the changing relationship between retailers and manufacturers: the use of global prices, terms and contracts, which are generally seen to be a manifestation of increased retailer power. The aim is to identify the legal consequences of replacing a series of nationally based supply contracts with one multinational or global arrangement.

CONTENTS

1. Commercial context 1

2. Recognition of the changing market dynamics and retailer buyer power 3

3. Legal background 8

4. Potential competition law obstacles to unified global supply contracts 11

Introduction 11

Pricing issues 14

Price discrimination 14

Retrospective rebates 19

Sales below cost 20

Vertical restraints 26

Resale price maintenance (RPM) 27

Refusal to supply 32

Refusal to stock/delisting 34

Slotting allowances and listing fees 36

Other promotional moneys 40

Abuse of economic dependency 41

5. Conclusion 43

Annex 44

1. COMMERCIAL CONTEXT

An examination of the developments in retailing will provide the necessary context and background to manufacturer–retailer relationships. The so-called 'retail revolution' has altered the balance of power between retailers and manufacturers in relation to branded goods, due to increased vertical integration of the distribution chain driven by the retailer.

This 'retail revolution' can be divided into four stages. The first was the development of retail chains; by 1980 five retailers accounted for 50 per cent of the market in many countries in Western Europe, although the structure of retailing varied considerably between the countries. This consolidation process then accelerated during the 1990s in part as a result of advances in information technology and the opportunities presented by economies of scale, and in part as a consequence of restrictive planning regimes impeding organic growth. This concentration process was aided by the second stage of the retail revolution which involved the development of large-scale shopping formats, ie the development of large out-of-town supermarkets and hypermarkets with surface areas in excess of 2,500m^2. The third stage of the retail revolution was the development of dedicated distribution systems by the large integrated retailers. Instead of relying on independent wholesalers, retailers started buying direct from manufacturers, storing products in their own distribution centres and taking responsibility for direct distribution to their retail stores. This in turn was influenced by the degree of retail concentration, so that the process occurred at different rates across the various countries. The final stage was the emergence of retailer brands as national brands in their own right.[1]

As the retail industry has consolidated, particularly across Western Europe, the smaller retailers have fallen by the wayside as large multinationals have thrived. A small number of large undertakings now generate the lion's share of retail sales in virtually all countries. The 80:20 rule applies: 80 per cent of sales are made from 20 per cent of stores. The arrival of Wal-Mart in Europe has ensured that the race among retailers to attain critical mass and economies of scale by mergers, joint ventures, and alliances will continue. While global buying scale is unproven, the fear that Wal-Mart will be able to make its global scale pay is a catalyst in the internationalisation of retailing.[2]

1 D Bell, 'The challenge of food distribution' in *The Global Food Industry: Strategic Directions*, ed Bill Ramsey for Financial Times Retail & Consumer (London: FT Business Ltd, 2000), pp 89–90.

2 C Maclure, *The Outlook for West European Retailing: a strategic insight into the issues, players and markets*, for Financial Times Retail & Consumer (London: FT Business Ltd, 1999), p 11.

Retailer buyer power stems partly from the range and diversity of products that the retailer stocks. Consequently, even though a supplier may have a considerable market share for a particular product, it may not be in a position to refuse a key retailer's demands. For the supplier, the retailer may represent a significant proportion of the supplier's overall sales but for a retailer this volume may only be a small percentage of its turnover. Thus power will shift to the retailer, especially as the retailer will have the option of switching between various suppliers, whereas for the supplier the retailer may represent one of its essential distribution outlets. Large branded goods manufacturers, whether global, European or national, rely on distribution through the majority of retail outlets; if access is denied to a retailer with 15 per cent of the retail grocery market, the supplier has lost access to 15 per cent of shoppers, since if the supplier's products are not available in that retailer's stores the shoppers are likely to buy an alternative branded or own label product, rather than switch stores just in order to find that single missing branded product.[3]

Buyer power is likely to arise when a retailer has either a dominant position in relation to the supplier (for example by virtue of exclusive supply arrangements), has strategic or leverage advantages, or has greater bargaining power resulting from its size or other characteristics. Whatever the reason, the result is that such a retailer will be able to obtain from the supplier conditions more favourable than those offered to competing buyers.[4]

[3] See, eg, paras 2.454 and 2.458 of the Competition Commission's Report, *Supermarkets: A report on the supply of groceries from multiple stores in the United Kingdom* (London: the Stationery Office, 2000) published on 10 Oct 2000 and paras 102–3 of the European Commission's decision in *Rewe/Meinl* 1999/674/EC: Commission Decision of 3 Feb 1999 relating to proceedings under Council Regulation (EEC) No 4064/89 (Case No IV/M.1221—*Rewe/Meinl*) OJ L 274 , 23 October 1999 pp 1–22.

[4] Paras 2.441 and 2.446-451 of the Competition Commission's Report on Supermarkets demonstrate that the larger the supermarket chain, the better the terms negotiated from suppliers. Conversely, smaller grocery retailers pay significantly more.

2. RECOGNITION OF THE CHANGING MARKET DYNAMICS AND RETAILER BUYER POWER

There has been a growing recognition of the changing dynamics in the retail sector, primarily as a result of the increasing concentration in retail markets. This has generated debate on the issue of buyer power, particularly with regard to the development of appropriate competition and anti-trust regulatory controls. Much of the literature has focused on the economic effects of increased retail concentration and buyer power as well as the ability of existing competition policy to regulate effectively without impeding the competitive structural evolution of retail markets.[5]

It should be noted that the concept of buyer power is not new. Indeed, in the United States, the enactment of the Robinson–Patman Act, prohibiting suppliers from offering preferential terms to selected buyers, was prompted by the growth of mass retailing in the 1930s. However, the criticism of such legislation and similar *per se* rules by partisans of a 'rule of reason' approach highlights the different ways in which the issue is being tackled in different jurisdictions. Consequently, while the concept may not be a new one for competition authorities, there is no clear general view in favour of or against buyer power.

At European level, the European Commission has produced a number of documents indicating its position on recent developments in the supply chain.[6] The Conference Papers of the European Competition Forum 1995 suggest that the participating competition authorities considered buyer power to be both a real issue and one that is open to exploitation. In particular, the discussions highlighted the difficulty of tackling the issue under traditional notions of anti-trust and competition law. Furthermore the Forum acknowledged the disparity in market concentration and retail structures in different countries as well as the current reality that most buying occurs at the national level, and went on to suggest that it was a topic therefore best left to national rather than EC regulation.[7]

[5] See eg OECD, *Buying Power of Multiproduct Retailers* (1999); Dobson, *Buyer Power and its Impact on Competition in the Food Retail Distribution Sector of the European Union prepared for European Commission* (1999); Dobson and Waterson, *Retail power: recent developments and policy implications* (Economic Policy, Apr 1998); London Economics, *Competition in Retailing* (1997). For a US policy perspective see, eg, Borghesani, de la Cruz and Berry, *Food for Thought: The emergence of Power Buyers and its Challenge to Competition Analysis* (1997). For EU policy see, eg, Vogel, *Competition Law and Buying Power: The Case for a New Approach in Europe* [1998] ECLR 4; Collins, *Retailer Buyer Power: Abusive behaviour and mergers/acquisitions* (Fordham: International Antitrust Law and Policy, 2000).

[6] Dobson Consulting, report prepared for the European Commission—DGIV Oct 1999, *Buyer power and its impact on competition in the food retail distribution sector of the European Union*, <http://europa.eu.int/comm/competition/publications/studies/bpifrs>.

[7] C D Ehlermann and L L Laudati (eds), *Proceedings of the European Competition Forum* (New York: John Wiley & Sons, 1997), Chapters 7–9.

The Commission's 1997 Green Paper on Vertical Restraints began a review process of its policy towards vertical restraints prompted in part by developments in the retail market, particularly increased retailer concentration and power resulting from size, globalisation and buying alliances.[8] The Green Paper recognised a shift in the traditional distribution process from manufacturer-push to consumer-pull and the expansion of the retailer's role in the supply chain. However, while the Commission recognised the concept of buyer power, it expressly excluded it from the scope of its detailed examination in the Green Paper.

Recent EC case-law has also recognised a development in the relationship between suppliers and large retailers. In the *Kesko/Tuko* decision, the Commission acknowledged the importance of considering the implications of these developments in its analysis of the proposed merger between two Finnish supermarket firms.[9] The decision was particularly significant because it recognised that in assessing the impact of the proposed merger, the definition of relevant market had to include both the downstream market (effect on consumers) and the upstream market (effect on manufacturers and suppliers), ie the market for the retailer's procurement of daily consumer goods. Furthermore, in assessing the retailer's exercise of its buyer power, the Commission recognised that a large retailer has a 'gatekeeper' function, determining who has access to both the procurement and consumer marketplace. By considering the transaction from the perspective of a retailer's influence over its suppliers, the Commission went beyond the traditional competition analysis of the downstream market implications of a merger. The significance of the decision was in the identification and consideration of the broader issues concerning the emerging dynamics of the retail marketplace, specifically an appreciation of the emergence of powerful retailers with the ability to exercise buyer power at different levels of the marketplace.

When examining the proposed acquisition of Promodès by Carrefour, the European Commission referred the analysis of a number of local retail markets to the national French competition authority (the *Conseil de la Concurrence*) at the request of the French government.[10] Meanwhile, the Commission authorised the acquisition, subject to a number of undertakings whereby Carrefour committed itself to remedying problems identified

[8] This review culminated in the new competition rules governing supply and distribution agreements: Commission Regulation (EC) No. 2790/1999 of 22 Dec 1999 on the application of Article 81(3) of the Treaty to categories of vertical agreements and concerted practices, OJ L 336, 29 Dec 1999, pp 21–5, and its accompanying guidelines, OJ C 291, 13 Oct 2000, which came into force on 1 June 2000.

[9] Commission Decision 97/227/EC *Kesko/Tuko*, OJ L 110, 26 Apr 1997. The Court of First Instance upheld the Commission's decision in its judgment in Case T-22/97 *Kesko v Commission* [1999] ECR II-3775.

[10] Conseil de la Concurrence: Avis n° 00-A-06 du 3 mai 2000 relatif à l'acquisition par la société Carrefour de la société Promodès.

in the procurement market. In particular, Carrefour committed itself to selling its 42 per cent stake in a competing retailer, Cora, to one or several independent competitors, following the Commission's conclusion that Carrefour's influence on Cora would have an anti-competitive effect on the market. Carrefour further undertook to abstain from modifying any supply contracts in force on the day of the Commission's decision for the remainder of their duration, in addition to a commitment not to delist certain producers supplying both Carrefour and Promodès for a period of three years from the date of the Commission's decision.[11]

This decision reflects the Commission's position in the *Rewe/Meinl* case, where the German food retailer Rewe (which had previously acquired the Austrian retailer Billa) was required to modify considerably its proposed takeover of the leading Austrian retailer Meinl, which would otherwise have given it a 37 per cent share of the Austrian retail food market. To avoid a prohibition decision, Rewe agreed to limit the takeover to about one-third of Meinl's business and accepted limitations in regions where the Commission argued that the merger would particularly strengthen Rewe's market power.[12]

The increased awareness of this new retail dynamic is further evidenced in a Commission publication on competition policy for the general reader.[13] There, the Commission refers to the retail merger cases listed above as examples of its merger policy and the document's 'Frequently Asked Questions' section uses the merger of two large supermarket chains as its first hypothetical example. This is an indication of the significance attached to the development of EU policy to deal with the emergence of this new manufacturer–retailer relationship.[14]

At national level, a number of initiatives have been launched by national competition authorities and governments in reaction to increased consolidation in the retail market. In France, the Government set up a round table initiative in January 2000 to review trade policy, which was followed by the introduction of a Bill (now enacted) on New Economic Regulations to expand some of the specific powers of the *Conseil de la Concurrence*, and to enhance the transparency of the merger control process.[15] Those measures

[11] Commission Decision of 21 Jan 2000 relating to proceedings under Council Regulation (EEC) No 4064/89 (Case No COMP/M.1684—*Carrefour/Promodès*) OJ C 164 of 14 June 2000, p 5. The Commission also referred the issue of Spanish retail markets to the Spanish competition authorities: see paras 34 and 108 of the decision. Also cf European Communities Commission: Press release of 26 Jan 2000, IP/00/74.

[12] See Commission Decision 1999/674/EC *Rewe/Meinl*, OJ L 274, 3 Feb 1999.

[13] EC Commission, *Competition Policy in Europe and the Citizen* (Brussels, 2000).

[14] See OECD report on 'Buying Power of Multiproduct Retailers' p 16 for the causes of retail sales concentration.

[15] Loi no 2001-420 du 15 mai 2001 relative aux nouvelles régulations économiques, JO Numéro 113 du 16 Mai 2001, p 7776. See in particular the projet de loi registered with the Presidency of the National Assembly on 15 Mar 2000 and there, in particular Exposé des motifs, Titre III: *Lutte contre les pratiques anticoncurrentielles*, Chapitre I, Orientations générales.

were prompted, in no small part, by the *Carrefour/Promodès* case and suppliers' complaints about the further consolidation of buyer power as a result of the creation of two 'super listing groups' (Opéra and Lucie).[16]

The UK's Office of Fair Trading has commissioned various studies examining the competitive effects of retailing and retailer buyer power as part of its research series on competition and consumer policy.[17] The reports highlight the new status of retailers as controllers of product distribution and as brand owners in their own right and recognise a shift in market power from manufacturers to retailers.[18] In addition, the reports consider various policy approaches for dealing with buyer power and the vertical restraint issues evidenced in modern retailing.[19]

Following a reference from the Office of Fair Trading under the Fair Trading Act 1973, the Competition Commission published a report in October 2000 on the supply of groceries from multiple stores—the culmination of a 16-month investigation.[20] The report largely exonerated the supermarket industry from accusations of excessive pricing, concluding that the industry is 'broadly competitive and . . . excessive prices are not being charged, nor excessive profits earned.'[21] Significantly, its recommendations for remedial action concerned relations with suppliers, for which a legally binding code of practice was proposed.[22] The report thus presents a useful insight into the regulatory approach to buyer power. The Competition Commission's recommendation of a code of practice was accepted by the government[23] and the code came into force on 17 March 2002.[24]

In Germany, even though the retail market is already highly regulated, there has been debate over whether the current state of retail concentration requires more extensive measures than the recent sixth amendment to the *Gesetz gegen Wettbewerbsbeschränkungen* (GWB—Act against restraints of competition), in order to prevent further concentration in the sector.[25]

[16] N McCarthy, 'The Jospin Government proposes new rules to curb retailer power' Issue 25 Mar 2000, *The European Retail Digest*.

[17] OFT, *Competition in Retailing Report* (1997); OFT: *Welfare Consequences of the Exercise of Buyer Power* (1998).

[18] OFT, *Competition in Retailing Report* (1997), pp 21–2.

[19] Broadly, these suggest that the competition authorities should be concerned with the competitive effect of the restraints rather than their form, and assessment should be made on a case-by-case basis. Nevertheless the analyses are clear in that the benign view of retailers formulated a decade ago is no longer appropriate.

[20] See n 3.

[21] Idem, p 7, para 1.13.

[22] The investigation disclosed a list of 52 practices whereby the supermarkets were found to have used their buyer power, Appendix 11.3 of the Competition Commission Report 2000, Vol 3.

[23] DTI Press release: *Byers publishes Competition Commission report on supermarkets*, P/2000/674 of 10 Oct 2000.

[24] Code of Practice on Supermarkets' Dealings with Suppliers attached to DTI press releases P/2001/606 of 31 Oct 2001; see also DTI press release P/2001/725 of 18 Dec 2001; and see text of Undertakings and Code of Practice in Annex hereto.

[25] In force from Jan 2000.

The tendency to favour increased regulation is illustrated by the decision of the *Bundeskartellamt* to develop its own principles for interpreting the German ban on sales below cost-price because the vague legal terms contained in the GWB provision have yet to be specified through administrative practice and court decisions.[26] The determination to regulate retail practices is further evidenced by the *Bundeskartellamt's* response to Wal-Mart's introduction of a range of budget products, where some items were sold below cost, threatening to fine the retailer for each item sold at an artificially low price.[27]

Developments in the US retail market, on the other hand, are perceived to lag behind the rapid concentration evidenced in Europe. The issue of buyer power and its effects have nevertheless begun to gain prominence as US competition authorities assess the significance of the change in retail dynamics. The Federal Trade Commission's hearing in 1995 on Global and Innovation-based Competition touched on competition aspects of market concentration in the retail sector while Congressional hearings of the Small Business Committee and the Committee on the Judiciary have considered the impact of super centres on small business and the issue of slotting allowances.[28] An FTC workshop in 2000 considered the competitive effects of slotting allowances and discussed the need for further regulatory measures, such as new Federal guidelines or other more restrictive measures.[29] The workshop presentations and discussions on enforcement policy regarding slotting allowances highlight both the significance of retailer market power in current policy debates and the problem of developing an appropriate regulatory response.

While there is a clear general recognition of the change in retail market dynamics and the potential competition effects this may generate, policy responses have emerged along national lines. Consequently these policy responses vary considerably from advocating strict regulation to a more *laissez faire* approach. It is these divergent regulatory approaches that will have an impact upon any global supply contract having effect across a number of different countries. It is to the legal problems that such contracts may encounter that this report now turns.

[26] Notice no 147/2000 of the *Bundeskartellamt* on the application of para 20(4), 2nd sentence GWB (sales below cost price).

[27] Beschluß B 9—74/00 *Wal-Mart Germany GmbH & Co. KG* of 1 Sept 2000. Cf BBC News online, 9 Oct 2000, *http://news6.thdo.bbc.co.uk/hi/english/business/newsid%5F963000/963617.stm*. Contrast Beschluß B 9–84/00 *Lidl Stiftung & Co. KG* of 1 Sept 2000 and Beschluß B 9–85/00 *Aldi Einkauf GmbH & Co. oHG* of 1 Sept 2000.

[28] House of Representatives Small Business Committee hearing 1994; 'Slotting Allowances and the Antitrust Laws' testimony of the FTC before the House Committee on the Judiciary, US House of Representatives, hearing on competitive issues in agriculture and the food industry, Washington DC, 20 Oct 1999.

[29] FTC public workshop on slotting allowances and other grocery market practices, 31 May–1 June 2000, Washington DC, *<http://www.ftc.gov/bc/slotting/index.htm>*.

3. LEGAL BACKGROUND

In order to determine the legal effects of manufacturer–retailer contracts in the different countries where goods are to be supplied, it is necessary to establish the likely content of a 'unified global supply contract'. The terms that could be envisaged in such a contract are dependent to a large extent on the commercial practicalities that underlie international supply transactions. This section outlines the broad issues to be considered in determining when and in what format unified global supply contracts could be used for the supply of particular products.

It is necessary to start out by considering the extent to which the structure involved in marketing and distributing a fast moving consumer good of necessity takes place at the *national* level, as this will affect the types of terms and conditions that could realistically be agreed in a global supply contract. With regard to marketing, it is important to note that the marketing of a branded good is the responsibility of the brand-owner, ie usually the manufacturer. Successful marketing of a brand is dependent upon the brand-owner building goodwill or 'equity' with the consumer. Indeed, that relationship would not exist if marketing were left to the retailer. Developing 'brand equity' with the consumer requires the supplier to have a national base in each country supplied in order to market the product in accordance with the relevant national (or local) consumer tastes and preferences. Thus the marketing element of the supply of fast moving consumer goods necessitates national marketing organisations to ensure that the product is pitched successfully in individual markets.

The distribution process may likewise necessarily involve national operations. This is dependent upon the degree to which the operation of the particular supply chain takes place internationally, nationally or locally. The supply chain functions consist of the **order**, the **invoice, delivery** and **payment. Ordering** tends to be a national operation because the replenishment process requires proximity to the point of sale. It is therefore rarely viable for ordering to take place on a global scale, particularly with regard to food retailing. In turn, **invoicing** for deliveries is also likely to take place locally or nationally, if the local operations are run as local profit centres in their own right. **Delivery** is predominantly a national operation, particularly in the case of food retailing. Products manufactured abroad will normally be delivered by the manufacturer or importer to the retailer's depot or warehouse, commonly called a regional distribution centre (RDC). **Payment** may take place either at the national or international level, depending upon the particular characteristics of the retailer. A central payment office, for example, would facilitate netting operations to minimise a retailer's currency exposure. As the Commission pointed out in

Rewe/Meinl,[30] the retailing trade (in Austria) 'obtains more than 80 per cent of its supplies from purely national suppliers . . . [T]he food retailing chains expect from producers services such as shelf maintenance and market research, which can be provided only through a presence on the spot.'

Furthermore, differing national consumer tastes will dictate product differentiation, both within and across national boundaries. This would presuppose a national or locally orientated supply process. Therefore both the marketing and distribution of branded products rely to a significant degree on national operations. Brand-owners require a national base for marketing purposes, while retailers are constrained by the logistics of the replenishment process, which through necessity operates at a national level. Overall, therefore, national actions will often underpin the global scope of retailers' activities. Once these issues are taken into account it is nevertheless possible to envisage a range of supply contracts that could be agreed at a global level.

At one extreme one could imagine a contract detailing the supply of a product at a single global net-net price. Commercial realities would however make such an agreement unlikely for the supply of a branded good. Widely varying cost structures in different countries for example make one global price financially impossible for most manufacturers of branded goods. The different factors that come into play include (i) national product regulations, such as ingredients and colours; (ii) national rules on sales promotions which may make certain packs (eg 3 for 2) unlawful and (iii) different distribution costs between densely populated and sparsely populated areas. The retailer, on the other hand, would run the risk of losing its competitive advantage in some markets by agreeing a single price for a branded product. An agreement on a single world wide net-net price is more likely to arise only in relation to the supply of retailers' own label goods by manufacturers.

At the other end of the scale would be an overarching global agreement, setting out only broad terms for the supply of a branded product whilst leaving the precise detail of the physical supply process to be negotiated at the national or local level. Such an agreement might be used by a central buying office to coordinate a retailer's relationships with its suppliers. The sort of terms envisaged in this type of agreement may refer to the product range to be supplied, the number of annual promotions, and perhaps a uniform growth bonus for which the supplier would offer the retailer a discount. In particular, terms such as growth bonuses would offer sufficient incentive to the retailer's central buying operation to promote the broader terms of the agreement to its local operators.

In between these two extremes there is a multitude of possible variations of terms that could be agreed at a global level to formulate the basis

30 See n 12, at paras 83–5.

of a global supply contract. One factor that will of course influence the actual terms agreed in individual circumstances is the relative strength and visibility of the manufacturer's brand balanced against the degree of leverage that the retailer is able to exert due to its scale. To highlight the various options, a selection of potential terms of varying contractual severity will be outlined briefly to provide the framework in which the consideration of the possible legal effects can be conducted.

Pricing terms offer a number of alternatives. It is for example possible for pricing terms to be broadly agreed at a global level but paid locally, according to differing national scales. The pricing terms negotiated are likely to refer not only to the invoice prices but also to discounts and promotional moneys. As indicated above, it is doubtful that there would be a term detailing a single global net-net price, given that this would be bound to undermine the retailer's competitiveness in some national markets. A more likely provision would be that the retailer would be supplied in all operating countries on 'best terms' ie a guarantee that the retailer benefits from terms no worse than those accorded by the supplier to the retailer's competitors in individual markets. A more problematic pricing term for the supplier would be the insistence by the retailer on a 'guaranteed margin', whereby if a competing retailer were to lower its retail price, the retailer would be able to match this price and demand that the supplier refund the difference. In the UK, it is likely that such unilateral demands would since 17 March 2002 be contrary to the Code of Practice regulating the relationship between the UK's four largest supermarkets and their suppliers.[31]

In addition to specific pricing terms, manufacturers in some cases pay retailers 'marketing moneys'. These generally consist of promotional moneys and advertising funds, and may include listing fees for store presence and slotting allowances for shelf-space and positioning of the manufacturer's product. Many of these practices (such as listing fees) would now be contrary to the UK Code of Practice. The payment of these marketing moneys will normally take the form of a reduction in the price charged by the supplier. As already mentioned, it is conceivable that broad parameters concerning the amount of marketing moneys to be paid could be agreed at the global level, leaving the precise details to be decided on a national basis. These marketing moneys present a major potential battleground between retailers and manufacturers; and retailers with powerful market positions will be likely to demand significant marketing moneys. Examples might in practice include: additional moneys for end of aisle displays; fixed end of year rebates in addition to discounts depending on volume of sales; the right to return unsold units; and demands for extended payment terms.

[31] See n 24.

4. POTENTIAL COMPETITION LAW OBSTACLES TO UNIFIED GLOBAL SUPPLY CONTRACTS

Introduction

This section will attempt to catalogue some of the major legal problems that may arise as a result of the implementation of a unified supply contract in the countries under consideration: the UK, France, Germany and the USA, taking into account the effect of relevant EU legislation.

A 'unified supply contact' is taken to mean a contract for the supply of goods which is made by a manufacturer/supplier with a retailer, where the goods are to be sold at retail level in more than one country. The actual terms of such a contract will be dependent upon the practicalities of the supply chain and the relative bargaining positions of the branded goods manufacturer as compared with the retailer. Therefore, the following examination will be based upon business practices likely to feature in such contracts. Rather than detail the regulatory regime in each of these countries, this report will select particular types of regulation likely to impact upon potential contractual obligations and other informal business practices. The section will concentrate on competition issues, as this is the primary focus of current or proposed regulation of manufacturer–retailer relations, and is especially relevant given the changing nature of market structure on which competition policy was developed. Furthermore, as the number and size of retailers operating in more than one country increases and transactions increasingly take place on an international scale, the focus of concern is on the likelihood of cross-border anti-competitive practices limiting competition and undermining the benefits of trade liberalisation.

First will be added some comments about free movement in EU law and treatment of the obstacles that national regulation and practice may represent under the case law of the Court of Justice on the free movement of goods.

National competition laws on unfair competition are a classic regulatory obstacle. However, for the EU review of national competition rules, the limitation of the scope of Article 28 EC in the early 1990s came at a critical point in time. The *Keck and Mithouard* decision by the European Court[32] and subsequent cases developing the limitation is important. The Court excluded a specific category of laws ('selling arrangements') from the prohibition of non-discriminatory restrictions. Only 'product requirements' would be covered by Article 28. The Court established that the regulation of selling arrangements, which does not imply any unequal treatment in law or in fact to the detriment of imported goods, could no

[32] Case C-267-268/91 *Keck and Mithouard*, 1993 ECR, I-6097.

longer be considered to restrict free movement. Other cases illustrate that 'selling arrangements' also include rules on advertising for goods.[33] However *Keck and Mithouard* and the limitation to 'product requirements' do not apply to the provision of services and the right of establishment. These freedoms may provide alternative grounds for review of national regulation.

Keck and Mithouard has not promoted a process of EU law review of national competition rules. Some of the ground may be re-conquered by the Commission, which has proposed new limitations in a Regulation on what member states can prohibit as unfair competition.[34]

An examination of competition issues that may arise as a result of global supply contracts must be set against a background of traditional competition analysis which has generally developed on the tacit presumption of **supplier** dominance, with the distributor, whether wholesaler or retailer, being regarded as in an inferior position in the relationship. Many competition laws in Europe, including the original EU block exemption for distribution agreements (1967), the UK Resale Prices (1976) and Restrictive Trade Practices Acts (1956 and 1976) and the German *Gesetz gegen Wettbewerbs-beschränkungen* (1957) were developed at a time when manufacturers largely dictated where and how their products would be sold. With the decline in the wholesaling function and the growth of retailers, manufacturers have lost their power to dictate the operation of the supply chain. Competition laws have of course developed and to some extent have reflected the change in balance of power and other structural changes in the way that goods are distributed. Thus the current EU block exemption (1999)[35], the orders made under the UK Competition Act 1998[36] and the new French law on economic regulation (2001)[37] to some extent have regard to the changing dynamics in the real world. The European Commission noted in its Green Paper on Vertical Restraints, the precursor to the block exemption, that 'the balance of power has clearly shifted towards retailers'. However, it is still the case that a retailer-imposed unified supply contract will be subject to some competition regulations that have been devised within a framework of very different market conditions.

[33] See Case C-292/92 *Hünermund* [1993] ECR I-6787 and Case C-412/93 *Leclerc-Siplec v TF1 and M6* [1995] ECR I-179.

[34] See Communication from the Commission on sales promotions in the Internal Market COM(2001) 546 final (2 Oct 2001) and the Proposal for a Regulation concerning sales promotions in the Internal Market.

[35] Commission Regulation (EC) No. 2790/99, 1999 OJL 336 and Guidelines on Vertical Restraints, 2000 OJ L 291.

[36] The Competition Act (Land and Vertical Agreements Exclusion) Order 2000, SI 2000 No. 310, and Vertical Agreements and Restraints, OFT 419, Mar 2000.

[37] Loi no 2001-420 du 15 mai 2001 relative aux nouvelles régulations économiques, JO Numéro 113 du 16 Mai 2001, p 7776.

Furthermore, the lack of a unified international competition law framework has resulted in different countries adopting differing approaches towards the enforcement and interpretation of anti-competitive practices by private business. Even within the EU a certain disparity remains between individual member states, despite closer harmonisation of national legislation and increased reach of EU legislation. This presents a number of potential complications for a single global contract that is to have effect across different countries. It is possible to envisage that unified trading terms will lead to business practices that do not comply with one or more national competition laws of the country where the goods are to be supplied, delivered, marketed or sold. In addition, if the supply of goods affects trade between countries, this may activate regional competition laws with which the business practices will also have to comply.

National and regional (especially EU) competition policy may target specific anti-competitive practices, which can be broadly categorised into regulations relating to **pricing issues, vertical restraints, horizontal restraints, abuse of dominant position** and **abuse of economic dependence.** Although this report does not intend to cover private label issues in depth, it is worth noting that the increase in private label goods also poses potential competition problems. Of primary concern to competition authorities will be the potential reduction in interbrand competition if smaller or weaker brands are delisted as a result of the introduction or growth of competing private label products. When a manufacturer sells both a branded product and a similar private label product there will be pressure on the manufacturer to give the retailer preferential terms for the private label product, or the retailer will not even purchase the branded product. However, the more common situation is that a private label product is manufactured by a supplier who does not, or has ceased to, supply branded products.

Own label suppliers commonly supply own label products to retailers on the basis of exclusive supply terms so that frequently the supplier is completely or partially dependent on the retailer.

A second possible competition problem arises when the retailer sells both a branded product and a directly competing product under its own 'brand' name. Supply of branded and competing own label products gives rise to the so-called 'customer-competitor' conflict:[38] the retailer, at one and the same time, has an arm's length contractual relationship with the manufacturer under which he agrees to display and sell the manufacturer's products to consumers, while at the same he (the retailer) is competing with the manufacturer by offering a directly competing own label product. The retailer has a conflict of interest in deciding *where* on the shelf to

[38] See, eg, para 112 of the Commission's Decision in *Rewe/Meinl* 1999 OJL 274.

place the branded product and his own label product, the *price* at which he sells both products, and how to *promote* the competing products.

The retailer faces a particular competition law dilemma in deciding how to price and promote his own label products given that he alone sets the retail price of both products and he has privileged access to the manufacturer's information about product innovations, promotions and factory pricing; the manufacturer does not of course have access to equivalent information about the retailer's competing own label products.

The next section will consider the competition issues likely to arise as a result of unified supply terms and will explore particular competition rules of the EU, UK, France, Germany, and the USA with which such contracts would have to comply.

Pricing issues

Pricing issues are the key feature in manufacturer–retailer relations, and will be a key aspect of negotiating unified trading terms. The principal competition considerations of unified pricing terms and practices will relate to the treatment of potential price discrimination and the effects of any sales below cost (loss-leading) or retrospective discounts accorded to retailers. In some instances pricing issues are directly linked to vertical issues, as manufacturers may instigate vertical restraints in order to counter the effect of retailers' pricing policies. These terms and practices may infringe national competition policies designed to protect smaller retailers from the competitive pressures of stronger competitors.

Price discrimination

The increasing internationalisation of retailers has brought pressure on pricing agreements negotiated with manufacturers as retailers seek to take advantage of price differentials for the same branded product in different markets. The demands of international expansion and international procurement are prompting retailers to attempt to extract global best pricing deals from their suppliers, whilst being careful not to forsake their local competitive advantage. If one retailer were successful in these negotiations, this would result in non-cost justified differences in treatment being accorded by the supplier to different buyers—ie price discrimination. Price discrimination may impact negatively on competition and efficiency in the retail market, particularly if buyers go beyond insisting on improved terms. Retailers with buyer power may be strong enough to interfere with suppliers' relations with rival retailers.[39] This could be achieved by requiring contractual commitments that

[39] OECD, *Buying Power of Multiproduct Retailers*, Background Paper by the Secretariat (Paris, 1999), p 21.

suppliers charge more to a retailer's competitors (or give the retailer concerned a better price than any of its competitors) or refuse to sell to them.[40]

In the United States, the Robinson–Patman Act (RPA) provides a strong law against price discrimination. Although the majority of the Act's provisions were orientated towards seller-induced activity, the prohibitions are also designed to prevent sellers acceding to the demands of large buyers. Thus, if the conduct or pricing activity resulting from a manufacturer-retailer agreement is subject to US antitrust laws, the RPA will apply to pricing and promotional concessions given to the retailer. A pricing agreement will be subject to the RPA to the extent that it has legal or practical consequences in the United States, which is usually the case where it is made or has effect there.

The RPA prohibits price discrimination, not price differences. Under Section 2(a), a seller is prohibited from discriminating in price between competing purchasers in contemporaneous interstate sales of goods of like grade and quality, if the price discrimination will result in adverse effects on competition. In theory this would not prevent global best pricing, provided that equivalent global pricing were available to similarly situated multinational customers. What needs to be considered, therefore, is the likelihood that the pricing agreements would be offered to only some multinational retailers ie only those retailers with sufficient buyer power. These retailers would then have a competitive advantage by being able to undercut the majority of their less powerful competitors on the goods in question, an advantage likely to be held to injure competition.[41]

The United States' Supreme Court decision in *FTC v Morton Salt*[42] makes clear that a pricing system will be illegal where it is available only to a limited number of buyers. The Court upheld the FTC's decision that selling to certain buyers for substantially less than the price offered to the buyer's competitors was harmful to competition. Therefore the principles of *Morton Salt* may preclude a manufacturer from establishing global best pricing or some other form of pricing policy to have effect in the United States, which could realistically apply to only a handful of large retailers and would give them a competitive advantage within the United States. In practice, however, it may be difficult to ascertain whether global pricing which, on its face, excludes the United States in fact gives large multinational retailers who have operations within the United States an advantage, through reduced *non-US prices*, that is in fact partially a function of their *US purchases*.

40 Refusal to supply will be considered in the vertical restraints section below.

41 See OECD report on 'Buying Power of Multiproduct Retailers', p 232 for the discriminatory concessions in favour of large buyers.

42 334 US 37 (1948).

United Kingdom

In the United Kingdom, the legal position with regard to price discrimination is now governed primarily by the Competition Act 1998 (CA 1998). The Office of Fair Trading (OFT) has issued a series of Guidelines of which the most relevant in the present context are:

- The Chapter I Prohibition (OFT 401)
- The Chapter II Prohibition (OFT 402)
- Market Definition (OFT 403)
- Assessment of Individual Agreements and Conduct (OFT 414)
- Assessment of Market Power (OFT 415)
- Vertical Agreements and Restraints (OFT 419)

Section 18(2)(c) of the CA 1998, mirroring at the national level Article 82(c) of the EC Treaty,[43] includes amongst the enumerated examples of the abuse of a dominant position,[44] which is prohibited by Chapter II of the CA 1998 and Article 82 EC, 'applying dissimilar conditions to equivalent transactions with other trading parties, thereby placing them at a competitive disadvantage'. As a result, where a dominant supplier charges different prices to different sets of customers, and these different sets of prices cannot be objectively justified, this has been held to constitute abusive conduct.[45] Charging the same price to all customers irrespective of differences in the costs of supplying them could equally amount to unjustified discrimination.

The implementation by a dominant manufacturer of global best pricing or other price discrimination policies, with the effect of distorting upstream or downstream competition, may therefore infringe the Chapter II prohibition. In the case of a dominant supplier, price discrimination which has the effect of distorting competition in the marketplace probably cannot be justified by the supplier on the ground that the supplier was simply responding to the wishes of its large customers.[46] A *non-dominant* supplier that *unilaterally* price discriminates does not infringe either the Chapter I prohibition, imposed by section 2 of the CA 1998, or Article 81

[43] Section 60 of the CA 1998 provides that the principles to be applied in determining questions under the relevant provisions of the Act shall include preservation of consistency of treatment under the Act with treatment under EC law.

[44] As market share of a correctly defined relevant market increases above 40 per cent, it becomes progressively easier to infer dominance, though the acid test is always whether, having regard to all the relevant circumstances, the undertaking possesses such *economic power* as to confer on it an exceptional freedom of action such as is not enjoyed by undertakings in normal competitive conditions: see generally Bellamy & Child, *Common Market Law of Competition*, 5th edn, Chapter 9, especially at paras 9-008 and 9-039 & ff.

[45] European Court of Justice decision in Case 27/46 *United Brands Continental BV v Commission* [1978] ECR 207.

[46] Cf Case T-65/89 *BPB Industries v Commission* [1993] ECR II-389; C-310/93P [1995] ECR I-865; and see n 26 above.

EC; a *non-dominant* supplier that agrees *with competitors* to price discriminate will infringe one or both of those prohibitions if the agreement has an appreciable economic effect; a *non-dominant supplier* that agrees with a *non-dominant customer* that the supplier will price discriminate will not infringe the prohibitions unless, even though neither party enjoys a dominant position, the market share of one or both of them is such (in excess of 30 per cent) that their agreement has an appreciable anti-competitive effect.[47]

Germany[48]

In Germany, in line with Article 82 of the EC Treaty, paragraph 19 of the GWB, as amended, directly prohibits the abuse of a dominant position. The definition of dominance in paragraph 19(2) provides that an enterprise has market dominance if there is no substantial competition or if the undertaking has a pre-eminent market position in relation to its competitors. There is a presumption of dominance where the enterprise has a market share of at least one-third of the relevant market.[49] The prohibition will apply to certain objectively unjustifiable restrictions of other enterprises, exploitation through unreasonable pricing polices, and other contractual or discriminatory terms which distort competition.

A dominant manufacturer in the relevant German market, operating a discriminatory pricing policy in favour of selected retailers, would be abusing its dominant position under German competition law if the policy falls within an established category of abusive practice deemed not objectively justifiable. Customers and potential customers disadvantaged by the pricing policy, who have suffered a competitive disadvantage as a result, can apply for judicial injunctions and can claim for damages.[50]

Paragraph 20(3) GWB contains a further provision prohibiting enterprises from using their market position, in the absence of objective justification, to put pressure on other undertakings to accord them preferential terms. This prohibition of procurement of discriminatory treatment applies to undertakings that occupy a dominant market position, including those in a dominant market position relative to their suppliers or customers, such that those undertakings are dependent upon them. While this regulation of

[47] Any contractual provision that infringes the Chapter I or II prohibition is void and unenforceable. And the infringing parties may be liable for third party damages and financial penalties of up to ten per cent of the turnover of the undertaking in the UK during the period of infringement (up to a maximum of three years): section 36 of the CA 1998 and The Competition Act 1998 'Determination of Turnover for Penalties' Order 2000, (SI 2000/309). OFT Guidelines: the Chapter II Prohibition (OFT 402).

[48] For the purpose of defining market dominance, the GWB provides that the market conditions within the relevant international markets are to be considered, irrespective of the question of the applicability of the Act to markets outside its scope.

[49] Para 19(4) GWB.

[50] Para 33 GWB.

relative market power remains controversial, not least because of the difficulties of defining relative market dominance, it suggests that the implementation of a pricing policy between a dominant retailer on the German market or one with relative dominance, and its supplier, granting the retailer non-cost justified preferential pricing terms, is likely to infringe this prohibition imposed by paragraph 20. If so, prohibition orders can be issued and civil law sanctions will apply, thus in principle enabling competing retailers to sue for an injunction or claim damages.

France

In France, competition rules aimed at balancing demand- and supply-side market power, particularly in relation to the retail industry, provide for the regulation of discriminatory pricing conditions through both abuse of dominance provisions and general prohibitions on discriminatory business practices. As in Germany, the prohibition of abusive conduct is extended to firms with relative market dominance in relation to dependent purchasers and suppliers, and market power is recognised not to depend entirely on market shares.[51] A discriminatory pricing policy may constitute an abusive practice under Article L. 420-2 of the newly integrated Code de Commerce, which specifies discriminatory business relations as an example of abusive conduct. If French competition rules apply to a manufacturer–retailer pricing agreement, whereby the manufacturer agrees to discriminate between customers on a non-cost justified basis, distorting downstream competition, this may constitute an abusive practice if the manufacturer is either dominant on the relevant French product and geographic markets, or has relative dominance. If the pricing policy infringes that prohibition, it will be void by virtue of Article L. 420-3.

A general prohibition of discriminatory sales and purchasing conditions, independent of the market position of the relevant undertakings is contained in Article L442-6 of the Code de Commerce. A discriminatory pricing policy that accords the retailer a competitive advantage, impairing downstream competition, is likely to fall within this general prohibition. Affected parties may bring claims for compensation and an injunction against the practice is possible.

European Community Law

Where the manufacturer–retailer pricing policy is subject to EU competition law, due to it affecting trade between Member States, it is likely that substantial price differentials between transactions of equivalent value will

[51] Article 8 Ordonnance no 86–1243 1986 relative à la liberté des prix et de la concurrence du 01-12-1986 (Order relating to freedom of prices and competition) now integrated into the Code de Commerce, Article L. 420-2.

be strong evidence of discrimination. This discrimination may infringe Article 82 of the EC Treaty, and could be prohibited, where the undertaking implementing the discriminatory policy holds a dominant position. Following the decision of the European Court of Justice in *United Brands v EC Commission*[52] it is unlikely that a manufacturer would be successful in using the defence that the discriminatory policy was forced on the supplier by the power of a dominant retailer. The court rejected this defence on the basis that, by definition, a dominant purchaser would be able to act independently of its suppliers. Therefore, a manufacturer with a dominant position within the EC market, or a substantial part thereof, may be abusing this dominance if it were to implement pricing practices available only to a small number of large retailers, in so far as they may affect trade between Member States.

Retrospective rebates[53]

Retailers may seek retrospective rebates. Such rebates may take the form of a volume incentive payment, a compensation payment where the retailer's profit on a manufacturer's product is less than expected, or a 'guaranteed margin' where the retailer has lowered its profit margin to match a competitor. The rebates will have the effect of retroactively reducing the price of the product to the retailer. Consequently, such rebates act as a form of price discrimination where they result in non-cost justified differences in treatment between different buyers. Such rebates adversely affect the competitiveness of the supplier and distort competition between both retailers and suppliers.

Where a unified supply agreement includes retrospective rebates that have the effect of distorting competition at the supply and/or retail level, the agreement may be subject to the competition rules regulating price discrimination described in the section above. This is the position in the USA where, in the FTC case *McCormick & Co*,[54] the complainant alleged that a spice-maker with a high market share violated the Robinson–Patman Act by granting discriminatory advantages to retailers, which included rebates and performance funds. Likewise, under UK, German, French and

[52] [1978] ECR 207.

[53] '. . . discount: the temporary offer of:
—a price reduction,
—an additional quantity of the identical good or service purchased which is offered at no additional cost to the purchaser,
—a coupon or voucher entitling a purchase of a good or service to a reduction on the price of an identical good or service on subsequent purchase'.

The 'Proposal for a Regulation of the European Parliament and the Council concerning sales promotions in the Internal Market' of the EU Commission, p 29.

[54] FTC File No. 961-0050. The company agreed to settle the FTC price discrimination charges arising under the Robinson–Patman Act; see FTC Decision and Order issued 27 Apr 2000, Docket No C-3939.

EU competition regulations, the grant of rebates may constitute abuse of dominance, so that a manufacturer with a dominant position would be abusing its position by implementing a discriminatory pricing practice that distorted competition.

In the UK, the Competition Commission's report on supermarkets identified retrospective rebates as a common practice that retailers use in their relations with suppliers. The Commission concluded that the practice, when carried out by retailers with buyer power, adversely affects the competitiveness of some of their suppliers, particularly small suppliers, and distorts competition between retailers in the supply of groceries, by disadvantaging those excluded from the scheme. It also distorts competition between suppliers by tending to insulate the major buyers receiving the rebates from risk, by transferring an undue element of that risk to the suppliers.[55]

The recommendation by the Competition Commission of a binding code of practice to regulate retailers' relations with suppliers proposed that the code should contain a provision that certain retailers should, amongst other prohibited activities, not seek any form of compensation for profits being less than expected.[56] The Competition Commission's recommendation, endorsed by the Secretary of State for Trade and Industry, was that those retailers with more than an eight per cent share of grocery purchases for resale from its stores in the UK should enter into a binding commitment to comply with the terms of the code.[57]

Sales below cost[58]

The practice of below-cost selling is a pricing strategy employed by retailers for certain products on which they will not be beaten in price, either because of a price pledge or because of a wish to maintain a certain price differential between themselves and their competitors. Alternatively, a retailer may sell particular products at a loss, because the offer of those products at an especially attractive price attracts extra trade in the store, including extra sales of other products on which the retailer earns a normal margin, with the result that the overall profit made by the store is increased. Loss-leading poses a problem for manufacturers because it may result in retailers who are not using the product as a loss-leader taking it off their shelves. In some cases it may also result in the consumer's perception of the

[55] Competition Commission, *Supermarkets: a report on the supply of groceries from multiple stores in the United Kingdom, Vol 1: Summary and Conclusions* (London: The Stationery Office, 2000), 2.495–2.497.

[56] Idem, 2.588 and para 6 of Code of Practice (see Annex hereto).

[57] Idem, 2.458 and see Annex.

[58] '. . . loss-leading is basically an advertising technique consisting of exceptionally low prices on a subset of retailers' goods'. OECD Report on 'Buying Power of Multiproduct Retailers', p 34.

quality of the product being diminished. Furthermore, retailers may seek to recoup their losses arising from consumers switching to below-cost products, by inducing manufacturers to reduce their list prices, even though it may be easier for retailers to absorb the loss through their sales mix. Manufacturers seeking to offset this practice by attempting to maintain minimum resale prices are likely to find themselves in conflict with laws against resale price maintenance (RPM).

Below-cost selling may amount to predatory pricing by a retailer if it extends beyond efficiencies consistent with competing profitably in a competitive market, and acts instead as a means to drive other retailers out of the market, subsequently enabling supra-competitive prices to be charged.[59] A further competitive concern identified by the UK's Competition Commission is the issue of cross-subsidy that occurs with sales below-cost. Large multiproduct retailers may be able to cross-subsidise loss-making products from revenues made from higher margin products, putting them at a competitive advantage relative to small and medium-sized competitors, especially if the latter are specialised.[60] Different national approaches have emerged to the regulation of below-cost selling. These range from laws specifically banning sales below cost to competition-based approaches prohibiting predatory pricing by dominant undertakings.

Germany

In Germany, paragraph 20(4) GWB directly bans below-cost selling. That provision states that the practice amounts to unfair hindrance of small and medium-sized enterprises where an undertaking with superior market power sells below cost price, with the exception of an occasional sale, unless there is an objective justification for doing so. Given that the vague legal terms used in the provision, such as 'cost price', have not yet been defined through administrative practice and court decisions, the *Bundeskartellamt* has begun the process of defining the concepts through developing principles of interpretation.[61] These stipulate the limits of permissible price competition in order to prevent intentional predation by powerful undertakings to the disadvantage of small and medium-sized competitors.

The principles enunciated by the *Bundeskartellamt* set out four criteria to be considered when examining whether a pricing practice comes under the prohibition set out in paragraph 20(4) GWB. First, the undertaking

[59] AKZO [1991] ECR I-3359.

[60] Competition Commission, *Supermarkets: a report on the supply of groceries from multiple stores in the United Kingdom, Vol 1: Summary and Conclusions* (London: The Stationery Office, 2000), 2.381.

[61] Notice no. 147/2000 of the *Bundeskartellamt* on the application of para 20(4), 2nd sentence GWB (sales below cost price).

under investigation must have superior market power in relation to its small and medium-sized competitors. Secondly, the sales below cost must not be merely occasional. This excludes from the scope of the prohibition one-off sales campaigns such as introductory prices, but specifies that offers over, or repeated during, a period of at least three weeks will not be classed as 'merely occasional', nor will long-running campaigns involving sales below cost of different items. The principles also aim to clarify the calculations involved in the BKA's determination of cost price. Thus, the basis for the calculations will be the supplier's list price, from which will be deducted all of the price-affecting terms contained in the supply contract, such as annual agreements, promotional moneys, etc. Finally, the BKA has explained its approach to the evaluation of what may amount to an objective justification of below-cost selling, balancing the interests of the company concerned with the interests of freedom of competition.

These principles of interpretation may enhance transparency in relation to the scope of the prohibition, but the precise calculation of cost price and the specific circumstances of each case will complicate proceedings. While the *Bundeskartellamt* may investigate allegations of below-cost selling, the decision whether to proceed with prohibition proceedings under paragraph 20(4) GWB will be dependent upon a comprehensive investigation of the specific circumstances of the undertaking involved. The decision not to initiate proceedings against the retail group Metro AG for selling below cost followed complex calculations of the cost price of various products and highlights the difficulty of determining whether the pricing practice falls foul of the prohibition set out in paragraph 20(4) GWB.[62] Conversely, the first prohibition decision under the ban, against Wal-Mart, Aldi Nord and Lidl for selling below cost price, indicates the *Bundeskartellamt's* willingness to fight unfair sales practices that are engaged in by undertakings with market power. There, the argument that the low prices were a reaction to similar price levels of other competitors was rejected as a justification for the below-cost pricing.[63] Consequently, pricing terms agreed between retailers and their suppliers are likely to come under scrutiny where the pricing strategy of the retailer with a presence on the German market appears to go beyond competitive pricing and becomes selling below cost.

France

French competition law similarly provides for a ban on selling at a loss, as part of its measures to limit retailer buyer power and to protect small shopkeepers from the competitive pressures of large retailers. Article L.

[62] *Bundeskartellamt*, 'No prohibition proceedings against Metro for selling below-cost price', press release, 27 Sept 1999.

[63] Decision of the *Bundeskartellamt* of 7 Sept 2000.

442-2 of the Code de Commerce expressly prohibits below-cost selling and related advertising. Retailers selling goods below cost price on the French market will be subject to a fine of up to FF 500,000 and the legal entity may be liable under the Penal Code according to Article L. 442-3.[64] In France the cost price is defined in Article L. 442-2 as the price listed on the invoice plus transportation costs and applicable taxes. Calculation of the cost price is made on the basis of data that are legally required to be detailed on the invoice.[65] The effect of this prohibition, in conjunction with further restrictive provisions regulating supplier–retailer relations, is that retailers cannot set retail prices below the invoice price for the goods and justify the practice by reference to off-invoice discounts, rebates or other allowances.[66]

In addition, as a complement to the ban on sales below cost, 'excessively low prices' are forbidden if their purpose is to restrict entry to the French market or to drive competitors out of business. Although the phrase 'excessively low prices' is not defined exactly in law, the intention is that the *Conseil de la Concurrence* will monitor prices that are low in comparison to production and distribution costs.[67] While this prohibition falls within the broader regulation of abusive conduct on the French market, which largely corresponds to European practice, the abusive pricing practice described in Article L. 420-4 is not dependent upon the market power of the undertaking concerned.

A retailer operating on the French market implementing a clear below-cost selling policy will be infringing the prohibition and faces financial penalties. However, prices which are not below cost but which appear to be excessively low may still be prohibited if, on the face of it, the intention behind the pricing policy is to exclude competitors. The fact that neither provision requires the retailer to have a dominant share of the French market is recognition that modern global retailers may wield buyer power without necessarily having traditional market dominance in the relevant product and geographic markets.

United Kingdom

Prior to the coming into force, on 1 March 2000, of the Competition Act 1998, suppliers could lawfully withhold goods from a retailer if the supplier had reasonable cause to believe that the retailer had been using the products as loss-leaders.[68] Under the new Chapter II prohibition,

64 Article L. 442-4 (I) Code de Commerce provides a list of exceptions to the ban on below-cost selling which includes end of season goods, perishable goods and food/non-food outlets of less than a specified capacity.

65 Article L. 441-3.

66 See section on vertical restraints below.

67 Article L. 420-5 Code de Commerce. This is a specific legal category targeting retailers' abuse of predatory pricing.

68 Resale Prices Act 1976 (now repealed) section 13.

charging prices which are below cost may constitute an abuse of a dominant position on a UK market, on the grounds that it is exclusionary, where the pricing strategy is aimed at eliminating competitors from the market.[69] Under the consistency principles set out in Section 60 CA 1998, the test for determining whether low pricing by a dominant undertaking is predatory or legitimate is that established by the ECJ in the *AKZO* case.[70] Applying that test, prices that are below average variable costs will be presumed to be abusive, whereas prices that are above average variable costs, but below average total costs (ie fixed costs plus variable costs), will be regarded as predatory if it can be established that the intention was to eliminate a competitor.[71] Therefore retailers instigating below-cost pricing in the UK may be guilty of abuse of dominance, but this will be dependent upon the retailer holding a dominant position in the relevant markets and a calculation that the loss-leading amounts to predatory pricing.

The report of the UK's Competition Commission on supermarkets investigated the practice of large multiples in the UK persistently selling certain products below cost. Although the Commission concluded that the practice distorted competition in the retail supply of groceries in the UK and operated against the public interest, it recommended no remedial action, stating that the remedies would in themselves have adverse effects disproportionate to the problem.[72]

European Community Law

Similarly, there is no general prohibition against sales below cost in European Community competition law. If the pricing practice is subject to EU competition rules by reason of the fact that it affects trade between Member States, it may constitute abusive conduct under Article 82 of the EC Treaty. Again this is dependent upon the existence of a dominant position and evidence that the pricing policy is predatory in the sense of having the aim of excluding competitors from the market, as per the test set out by the ECJ in the *AKZO* case.[73]

USA

There is no explicit prohibition of the sale of goods below cost in the

[69] Section 18(2) CA 1998, mirroring Article 82(c) EC Treaty.

[70] [1991] ECR I-3359.

[71] The rules of thumb enunciated by the ECJ are necessarily subject to exceptions where there is an objective justification for the below-cost retail sale, eg most obviously, in the present context, where the product is approaching its sell-by date and the retailer deems it better to get something than to risk getting nothing for it.

[72] Competition Commission, *Supermarkets: a report on the supply of groceries from multiple stores in the United Kingdom, Vol 1: Summary and Conclusions* (London: The Stationery Office, 2000), 2.558.

[73] Case 62/86 [1991] ECR I-3359.

United States. Where there are concerns over the monopolisation of markets and the elimination of market competition, which are prohibited under Section 2 of the Sherman Act, the existence of below-cost selling may be used as evidence of monopolisation. However, according to a decision of the US Supreme Court in *Brook Group Ltd v Brown Williamson Tobacco Corp*, Section 2 is infringed only if there is a likelihood that the undertaking concerned could recoup the losses incurred from loss-leading through subsequent monopoly profits.[74] The Court did not, however, specify the appropriate criteria for assessing costs. Further case-law has laid down additional conditions for establishing unlawfulness of sales below cost price. In *Wal-Mart Stores, Inc v American Drugs, Inc* the Arkansas Supreme Court rejected the plaintiffs' argument that Wal-Mart's practice of selling certain pharmacy items below the wholesale cost, and its advertising statement that it would never be undersold on a pharmacy item, violated State law on predatory pricing.[75] At first instance the Chancery Court cited circumstantial evidence when inferring that Wal-Mart possessed the requisite intent to injure competitors and distort competition. That evidence relied on Wal-Mart's pricing and promotional policies. The Arkansas Supreme Court overturned the lower court's decision, ruling that the lower court had improperly inferred predatory intent from Wal-Mart's tactics, which the State Supreme Court considered were consistent with healthy pro-competitive activity, and stated that the Arkansas law did not make loss-leading illegal.

The ruling is consistent with Federal predatory pricing laws that permit below-cost selling and require the courts to examine whether loss-leading harms overall competition, rather than whether the practice harms individual competitors.[76] However, there is a considerable difference of approach between Federal and State laws in the USA with regard to predatory pricing. While Federal laws are concerned with overall competition in the market and apply a 'rule of reason', State laws tend to focus on the protection of competitors and do not require actual proof of anti-competitive intent for a finding of illegality.[77] To date, no other predatory pricing suits have been filed under State laws, but if a loss-leading practice, similar to that in the *Wal-Mart* case, were held to be illegal, similar challenges might well emerge across the rest of the USA, thereby making it increasingly difficult for retailers wishing to engage in loss-leading to implement a nation-wide pricing strategy.

[74] 509 US 209 (1993)

[75] 319 Ark 214, 891 SW 2d 30 (1995).

[76] See US Supreme Court in *Matsushita Electrical Industrial Co v Zenith Radio Corp* 475 US 574 (1986).

[77] W Borghesani, P de la Cruz, and D Berry, *Food for thought: the emergence of power buyers and its challenge to competition analysis* (Washington DC, 1997), *<http://www.antitrust.org/economics/vertical/grocery/FOOD.htm>*, p 25.

The different approaches of the various jurisdictions highlight two major issues facing retailers wishing to implement below-cost pricing on certain products in various markets. The first is the issue that calculations of the cost price will vary according to the approach of the competition authority concerned, which is particularly significant for retailers operating in jurisdictions where below-cost selling is prohibited. Consequently, various reductions or other terms granted to the retailer as a lump sum payment may be taken into account in one jurisdiction but not another. Second is the issue of whether a low pricing strategy will be considered to be anti-competitive. Different competition authorities and courts may interpret specific practices of below-cost selling very differently. In one jurisdiction loss-leading may be interpreted as a pro-competitive practice, even where it is used by retailers with buyer power. In other jurisdictions, below-cost selling may be *per se* illegal or may be considered evidence of an abusive practice. Insofar as a retailer wishes to preserve flexibility to price downwards and wishes to get a supplier to bear or share the cost to the retailer of so doing in certain circumstances, the divergences of approach from one jurisdiction to another noted above will, at the very least, greatly complicate global manufacturer-retailer pricing agreements.

Vertical restraints

In the past, the majority of vertical restraints were imposed by manufacturers on retailers and accordingly much of the policy and economic analysis relating to vertical restraints was developed by reference to a manufacturer-push economic model. The recent and rapid expansion in size and market power of a number of retailers has led to consumer-pull markets, and consequently the balance of competitive power has shifted to retailers. The large powerful retailer now often has the upper hand, and is more able to instigate upstream vertical restraints. As a result, vertical restraints are being used by both retailers and manufacturers to maximise their interests. For retailers, they are a means of exercising greater control over manufacturers' activities, while manufacturers may use vertical restraints as a counter-balance to retailers' buying power and to prevent retailers benefiting from an unfair competitive advantage as a result of being both customers and competitors.[78] Given that it is becoming increasingly difficult to distinguish between vertical intervention and vertical integration now that buyer power accords retailers considerable influence over manufacturers' investment and production decisions, and the fact that traditional vertical restraints may not be employed for traditional reasons, it is important to examine the ways in which retailers and manufacturers

[78] This dual 'customer-competitor' conflict is the result of retailers selling competing private label goods: see n 38.

actually intervene in each other's behaviour rather than examine the traditional vertical restraints themselves.

A global supply contract imposing vertical restraints, whether instigated by the retailer or the manufacturer, may be simultaneously subject to different national competition policies. The analysis of vertical restraints in one jurisdiction may be based on the historic presumption of supplier dominance, while another national policy may focus instead on the competitive effects of the restraint at both retailer and manufacturer market levels, if one or more of the firms possesses market power.[79] The varying policies may lead to anomalous results.

There are numerous vertical restraints that could be envisaged between retailers and manufacturers. The UK's Competition Commission report identifies various restraints employed by UK retailers in their dealings with suppliers. The findings illustrate that the practices may be the result of formal contractual obligations or, more commonly, the result of 'off-contract' negotiations. The Competition Commission's comprehensive study, along with others,[80] suggests that vertical restraints between retailers and manufacturers (sometimes bilateral contractual commitments, but sometimes unilateral acts by one of the parties within the context of a continuing vertical trading relationship) might include: refusal to supply, resale price maintenance, tying arrangements, refusal to stock (delisting), minimum advertising requirements, slotting allowances and listing fees.

Resale price maintenance (RPM)

As mentioned in the section, above, regarding sales below cost, manufacturers may wish to maintain minimum resale prices in order to counter the effects of retailer loss-leading practices. However, the use of minimum RPM is considered to be an anti-competitive price-fixing mechanism, and as such the practice violates competition regulations across all of the jurisdictions considered in this report. The setting of maximum or recommended resale prices is generally unobjectionable and one of the reasons for adoption of those practices may be that the retailer has private label goods and the supplier of the national branded product does not want the retailer to overprice the latter in order to make private label goods appear to be better value. From a competition perspective, maximum RPM is less likely to be a problem since it allows retailers to compete by charging

[79] Paul Dobson and Michael Waterson, 'Vertical Restraints and Competition Policy', Office of Fair Trading Research Paper 12 (UK, Dec 1996), pp 50–2.

[80] See, eg, London Economics, 'Competition in Retailing', Office of Fair Trading Research Paper 13 (UK, Sept 1997), p 40; OECD, *Buying Power of Multiproduct Retailers*, Background Paper by the Secretariat (Paris, 1999), pp 37–9; Dobson Consulting, report prepared for the European Commission—DGIV Oct 1999, *Buyer power and its impact on competition in the food retail distribution sector of the European Union*, <http://europa.eu.int/ comm/competition/publications/studies/bpifrs>, pp 96–7, 117–18, 133.

lower prices, provided that it is not used to facilitate collusion among retailers.[81]

Germany

In Germany, both maximum and minimum RPM is prohibited despite the generally positive treatment afforded by German law to vertical restraints, which are permissible *per se* except where they infringe EC competition law. Following the introduction of the 6th amendment to the GWB, the new paragraph 14 prohibits agreements between undertakings that restrict the free determination of prices or business terms *vis-à-vis* third parties, relating to markets to which the Act applies.

The GWB prohibits not only both minimum and maximum resale prices, but also, by paragraph 22 (1), recommendations, including recommendations of retail prices, which through uniform application would circumvent prohibitions set out in the Act or decisions taken by the *Bundeskartellamt* pursuant to the Act. However, paragraph 23 of the GWB exempts non-binding price recommendations issued by an enterprise for the resale of its branded goods, if the goods are in price competition with similar goods of other manufacturers. Such recommendations must be expressly designated as non-binding, and no economic, social or other pressure may be applied to enforce them.[82] A branded goods manufacturer attempting to influence resale prices that will affect the German market will be prohibited from doing so unless the pricing terms negotiated with retailers are non-binding and purely recommendatory in nature.

France

Under French law, RPM is prohibited by means of two inter-linking provisions in the new Code de Commerce. Article L. 442-5 provides for fines of FF 100,000 for anyone imposing minimum resale prices, whether directly or indirectly. That prohibition must be read in conjunction with Article L. 420-1.[83] This Article provides that any concerted action that distorts the free determination of resale prices in the French market is prohibited. Therefore it is unlawful for suppliers to impose either minimum or maximum resale prices where these will lead to uniform prices being applied by the retailer. Consequently, for the purposes of Article L. 442-5 it may be irrelevant whether the resale price is either minimum or maximum, given that Article L. 420-1 regulates the anti-competitive price-fixing effect resulting from uniform price application. Recommended resale prices, however, will be lawful provided that they are non-binding, allowing the

[81] For the ban on price recommendations, see OECD Report on 'Resale Price Maintenance', p 69.

[82] Para 23(1) GWB.

[83] For a brief examination of the provisions applicable in France, as to the RPM, see OECD Report on 'Resale Price Maintenance', p 59.

retailer the freedom to determine the final resale price. Suppliers imposing maximum RPM on goods to be sold in the French market will be constrained to the extent that the pricing agreement may not have anti-competitive effects on the French market.

United Kingdom

In the UK, minimum RPM falls within the Competition Act 1998 Chapter I prohibition covering anti-competitive agreements. Although an agreement is unlikely to be considered to have an appreciable effect on competition where the combined market share of the parties is less than 25 per cent, this market share cap is not extended to minimum RPM agreements.[84] Suppliers imposing minimum resale prices on retailers operating in the UK will be infringing the Chapter I prohibition regardless of their market share.

On the other hand, maximum or recommended resale prices may be permitted under the Competition Act 1998 (Land and Vertical Agreements Exclusion) Order 2000—the 'Exclusion Order'.[85] Following the lead of the European Commission, the UK has decided to exclude vertical agreements from the scope of the Chapter I prohibition, and has modelled the Exclusion Order on the European Commission Vertical Restraints Block Exemption.[86] However, the UK Exclusion Order omits the 30 per cent market share threshold above which the EC Regulation is inapplicable, as well as omitting the hardcore restrictions that are excluded from the scope of the EC Regulation. The only equivalent restriction contained in the UK Exclusion Order that would take a vertical agreement outside its scope relates to price-fixing. Thus, the Exclusion Order provides that the exclusion for vertical agreements does not apply to any vertical agreement which directly or indirectly has the object or effect of restricting a buyer's ability to determine its sale price. Agreements where the seller imposes a maximum or recommended sale price may benefit from the exclusion except where such a maximum or recommended sale price results, in practice, in a fixed or minimum sale price because of pressure from, or any incentives offered by, any of the undertakings involved. Where recommended or maximum prices have such an effect the agreements will not benefit from the exclusion for vertical agreements.[87] Examples of types of practices that may result in fixed or minimum sale prices include:

[84] Office of Fair Trading: *Director General of Fair Trading's Guidelines: The Chapter I Prohibition*, OFT 401 (Mar 1999), paras 2.19–2.20, reprinted in G Lindrup (ed), *Butterworth's Competition Law Handbook*, 6th edn (London: Butterworths, 2000), p 341.

[85] SI 2000 No 310.

[86] Commission Regulation No 2790/1999.

[87] Office of Fair Trading: *Director General of Fair Trading's Guidelines: Vertical Agreements and Restraints Guidelines*, OFT 419 (Feb 2000), para 3.2.

- Agreements fixing the maximum level of discount a distributor can grant;
- Intimidation, delay or suspension of deliveries and contract terminations in relation to the observance of a certain price level; and
- Measures aimed at identifying price-cutting distributors, such as the implementation of a price monitoring system.

Where the supplier is dominant, even the mere unilateral recommendation of a resale price is in principle capable of being scrutinised to establish whether it might lead to collusion between the supplier's retail outlets, and the same is true of the imposition of a maximum resale price.[88]

European Community Law

RPM agreements, which are subject to EC competition rules, fall to be considered under the European Commission Vertical Restraints Block Exemption Regulation.[89] The exemption provided by the Regulation does not apply to vertical minimum price-fixing agreements, whether direct or indirect, which remain a violation of Article 81(1) of the EC Treaty under all circumstances.[90] The Commission makes clear that this does not prohibit maximum RPM or recommended resale prices that are not enforced in practice. Permitting maximum RPM represents a change in Commission practice, indicating that it is moving towards a 'rule of reason' approach.[91]

The Commission's Guidelines on Vertical Restraints detail the extent to which recommended and maximum resale prices are permissible.[92] A maximum resale price will be covered by the Block Exemption Regulation where the market share of the supplier does not exceed 30 per cent.[93] For cases above this market share threshold, the Guidelines identify two potential anti-competitive effects associated with recommended and maximum resale prices. The first is that the practice may result in the majority, or all, of the *retailers* following the recommended or maximum resale price. The second identified risk is that such resale prices may facilitate collusion amongst *suppliers*. According to the Guidelines, the means of assessing those possible anti-competitive effects should be based primarily on the market position of the supplier. Thus, the stronger the brand of the

[88] See, eg, para 227 of the Commission's Guidelines on Vertical Restraints (which suggests that recommending resale prices or setting maximum prices by a strong supplier may lead to collusion contrary to Article 81).

[89] No 2790/1999.

[90] Idem, Article 4(a).

[91] For an exemption of book RPM from EU Competition rules, see OECD Report on 'Resale Price Maintenance', p 110.

[92] European Commission: *Commission Notice—Guidelines on Vertical Restraints*, OJ C 291 of 13 Oct 2000, p 1.

[93] Idem, point 225.

supplier, the higher the risk that a recommended or maximum resale price will lead to a more or less uniform application of that price level by retailers keen to stock that particular brand. The market position of competitors should also be taken into account when assessing the anti-competitive effects of this pricing practice. The Guidelines suggest that where a narrow oligopoly exists, recommended or maximum resale prices may facilitate collusion between the suppliers through the exchange of pricing information, thereby reducing the likelihood of lower resale prices. Where the implementation of recommended or maximum resale prices leads to such effects, they will violate Article 81(2) of the EC Treaty.[94] Supply contracts containing recommended or maximum resale price provisions that will affect trade between Member States will receive an exemption in relation to Article 81(1) where the supplier falls under the 30 per cent market share threshold. Above this limit the practice will be investigated and, if found to be anti-competitive, will be prohibited.

USA

The USA has also witnessed a relatively recent change in its approach to RPM. All RPM agreements are capable of attracting the prohibition of the Sherman Act. Following the decision in *Albrecht v Herald Company*,[95] in which the US Supreme Court held that maximum vertical price-fixing was a per se antitrust violation, case-law proceeded on the basis that both maximum and minimum RPM were *per se* illegal. The prohibition included agreements whereby the resale price was agreed between the buyer and the seller, as well as instances where the seller forced the purchaser to sell at the stated price. However, recommended resale prices were permissible under the decision of the Supreme Court in *United States v Colgate & Co.*[96] Considerable criticism of *Albrecht's* theoretical justifications for *per se* illegality of maximum vertical price-fixing and the increased irrelevancy of the decision to antitrust enforcement under the Sherman Act resulted in the decision being overruled by the US Supreme Court in *State Oil Co v Kahn*.[97] The Court noted that this did not imply that all vertical price-fixing is *per se* lawful, but simply that it should be evaluated under the 'rule of reason' approach, which would effectively identify those situations in which it amounts to an anti-competitive practice. Consequently, suppliers instigating RPM on the US retail market may do so provided that the price-fixing does not amount to minimum RPM or have an anti-competitive effect on the US market.

[94] Idem, points 226–8.

[95] 390 US 145 (1968).

[96] 250 US 300 (1919).

[97] 96-871 (1997).

Refusal to supply

Refusal to supply was traditionally used by manufacturers to counter below-cost selling and prevent free-rider problems amongst retailers. It is now becoming more common for those retailers with buyer power to instigate refusal to supply by demanding that manufacturers refuse to supply certain other competing retailers.[98] The resulting exclusive supply of a branded product may restrict or distort competition between retailers to the extent that those retailers that do not have access to the product are at a competitive disadvantage. However, the investigation into practices between suppliers and multiple stores carried out by the UK Competition Commission suggests that, at least in the United Kingdom, retailer-instigated refusal to deal is effectively limited to private label goods.[99]

France

In France they have now opened up for a refusal to supply, so that it is permitted in most areas. Under the old *Ordonnance* relating to freedom of prices and competition, a manufacturer would have been liable for damages if it refused to supply a purchase order which was neither unusual nor made in bad faith.[100] The change was brought about by the introduction of the 1996 Loi Galland, the purpose of which was to reduce the imbalance between suppliers and retailers by limiting retail chain buyer power.[101] The new right of manufacturers to refuse to supply does not however affect food retailing, see further on page 35.

United Kingdom

In the UK manufacturers with a dominant position on the UK market may be obliged to supply retailers, because a refusal may constitute an abuse of dominance under the Chapter II prohibition. Applying the case-law of the European Court of Justice, refusal by a dominant undertaking to supply an existing customer can be an abuse if there is no objective justification for the refusal.[102] The OFT has indicated that possible justifications for refusal to supply might include the prevention of free-riding, the existence of a selective distribution system and capacity constraints that physically

[98] London Economics, *Competition in retailing*, Office of Fair Trading Research Paper 13 (UK, 1997), p 40.

[99] Competition Commission, *Supermarkets: a report on the supply of groceries from multiple stores in the United Kingdom, Vol 1: Summary and conclusions*, (London: The Stationery Office, 2000), 2.487.

[100] Article 36(2) Ordonnance no 86-1243 1986 relative à la liberté des prix et de la concurrence du 01-12-1986.

[101] Loi no 96-603 du 5 Juillet 1996 relative au développement et à la promotion du commerce et de l'artisanat, now integrated into the new Code de Commerce.

[102] *Commercial Solvents v Commission* [1974] ECR 223.

prevent supply.[103] It is likely that a refusal to supply by a manufacturer with a market share of over 40 per cent of the relevant UK market will be regarded as abusing a dominant position in breach of the Chapter II prohibition if there is no objective justification for the refusal.

Retailer-instigated refusal to deal, as a means of exercising greater control over manufacturers, may result in a foreclosure of the market where it excludes existing or potential competitors on the demand side. This would give rise to competition concerns in respect of the exclusive supply of branded goods. However, the findings of the Competition Commission's report on supermarkets suggest that, at least in the United Kingdom, requiring exclusive supply of a product is generally limited to private label goods. In this respect the Competition Commission concluded that the practice did not adversely affect the competitiveness of suppliers or distort competition between suppliers in the supply of groceries.[104] An exclusive supply term relating to private label goods or providing for exclusivity over a limited period for the introduction of a new product would be unlikely to constitute an anti-competitive restraint under UK competition rules.

European Community law

EU competition rules do not impose a duty to supply. Instead, Article 82 of the EC Treaty effectively imposes a duty on dominant firms to behave responsibly, especially towards those dependent on the undertaking in order to continue trading. Case law provides that a dominant undertaking may be obliged to supply products to other parties, unless there is an objective justification for not doing so. A refusal may amount to an abuse of a dominant position. In *Boosey & Hawkes*, the Commission declared that a sudden withdrawal of supplies might constitute abusive conduct.[105] This was stated most forcefully in the *United Brands* case, where the European Court of Justice held that it was an abuse of a dominant position for United Brands to cease supply of bananas to a Danish banana ripener.[106] A dominant manufacturer instigating a refusal to supply in order to counter retailer practices, such as loss-leading, risks abusing its dominant position within the EU market where trade between Member States is affected. It is doubtful whether loss–leading would justify a refusal to supply in order to satisfy the requirement that the refusal be indispensable to the alleged justification.

103 Office of Fair Trading: *Director General of Fair Trading's Guidelines: The Chapter II Prohibition*, OFT 402 (Mar 1999), para 4.47, reprinted in *Butterworth's Competition Law Handbook* (6th edn, 2000), p 356.

104 Competition Commission, *Supermarkets: a report on the supply of groceries from multiple stores in the United Kingdom, Vol 1: Summary and conclusions* (London: The Stationery Office, 2000), 2.487.

105 [1988] 4 *CMLR* 67.

106 *United Brands Continental BV v Commission* (27/76) [1978] ECR 207.

The Block Exemption Regulation No 2790/1999 will apply across all sectors so that vertical restraints instigated by retailers will receive the same treatment as those instigated by manufacturers. A retailer-induced exclusive supply term will be treated as neither always prohibited nor freely permitted. Instead it will be subject to market share rules, such that below the 30 per cent threshold, the retailer may benefit from the exemption in relation to the Article 81(1) prohibition, but above this level, the practice will be investigated by the Commission and, if necessary, prohibited.

USA

In the USA individual refusals to deal are not *per se* illegal.[107] Refusals to supply will be lawful provided that the manufacturer acts independently. The US Supreme Court has stated that, 'a manufacturer . . . generally has a right to deal, or refuse to deal, with whomever it likes, as long as it does so independently.'[108] However, collective refusals to deal with third parties may be deemed illegal. This would prevent suppliers boycotting a particular retailer, for example in protest at the supply terms and resale pricing practices of the retailer.

Refusal to stock/delisting

A retailer may threaten not to stock a supplier's products in order to get the supplier to agree to particular supply terms and conditions. With regard to leading brands, it is argued that the practice is relatively rare. Customer demand obliges retailers to stock these so-called 'must-stock' brands.[109] Manufacturers of strong brands are therefore in a better position to resist retailer demands to comply with supply terms, whether contractual or not. However, while delisting or refusing to stock a must-stock brand is unlikely, a retailer can cause damage by delisting particular pack sizes or varieties of a branded product. Smaller suppliers, suppliers of generic goods and those supplying private label goods to retailers, are in a comparably weaker position *vis-à-vis* the retailers, as they may be dependent upon them as an outlet for their products. Consequently such suppliers are under greater pressure to comply with retailer demands when faced with a threat of delisting. The Competition Commission's report on supermarkets indicated that where the delisting of a branded good was not

[107] Section 1 of the Sherman Act.

[108] *Monsanto v Spray-Rite Service Corp*, 465 US 752, 761 (1984), citing *United States v Colgate & Co*, 250 US 300, 307 (1919).

[109] Dobson Consulting, report prepared for the European Commission—DGIV Oct 1999, *Buyer power and its impact on competition in the food retail distribution sector of the European Union*, <http://europa.eu.int/comm/competition/publications/studies/bpifrs>, p 107.

linked solely to product quality, the practice may lead to a distortion of the supplier market.[110]

Refusal by a retailer to stock particular goods may be subject to the rules regulating refusals to deal in general. Most of the experience in the USA, UK and the EU refers to a refusal by a seller to deal with a particular customer. However, the same criteria should apply to a powerful retailer who is the primary outlet for product sales in a particular local market.

Germany

In Germany the rules prohibiting boycotts and other restrictive practices under paragraph 21 GWB will similarly regulate the legality of retailer delisting practices. A retailer will be prohibited from delisting a supplier, or threatening to do so, as a means of forcing the supplier to act in a way that, were it the subject of an agreement between the supplier and the retailer, would be prohibited by the GWB: eg, discriminatory pricing or treatment and other competition-distorting practices.[111]

France

Retailers operating on the French market who threaten suppliers with delisting, or do so in practice, may be abusing a dominant position or could be liable under a general prohibition. Actual refusal to stock on the sole ground that the other party will not submit to unjustified business conditions will constitute an abusive practice under Article L. 420-2 of the Code de Commerce, where either the retailer is dominant on the relevant French markets, or if other firms are economically dependent upon it. Any contractual clause providing for delisting if certain business terms are not met will be void under Article L. 420-3. The threat of a sudden breaking-off of commercial relations, which covers delisting, in order to seek unjustified commercial advantages, including preferential prices, payment delays or other discriminatory trading terms, is prohibited under Article L. 442-6(I)(3). This general prohibition operates independently of the market position of the undertaking concerned. A retailer seeking to coerce suppliers into agreeing to disproportionate supply conditions which will affect the French market is prohibited from threatening delisting and may be prohibited from delisting in practice where it is either dominant or has relative dominance *vis-à-vis* its suppliers. The New Economic Relations Law implements new rules to curb abusive delisting by retailers.

[110] Competition Commission, *Supermarkets, a report on the supply of groceries from multiple stores in the United Kingdom, Vol 1: Summary and Conclusions* (London: The Stationery Office, 2000), 2.520; the Code of Practice (see Annex) adopted in consequence of the report prohibits listing fees except for new product lines.

[111] Paras 21(2) and (3) GWB.

Slotting allowances and listing fees

Slotting allowances and listing fees are payments, both initial and annual, to retailers by manufacturers with a view to placing and retaining particular products on retailers' shelves, as well as payments to secure preferential shelf-space within particular stores. The existence of such fees and allowances can affect both competition among manufacturers of established brands and competition among retailers. Dominant manufacturers able to offer high slotting allowances in exchange for 'exclusives', whereby rival manufacturers are excluded, will exclude existing and potential competitors unable to match those fees. Even without 100 per cent exclusivity, a manufacturer may be able to marginalise its competitors and lessen the amount of competition it faces through the payment of fees that guarantee the manufacturer a large percentage of shelf-space or a right of veto over other manufacturers' products. However, a manufacturer able to gain shelf place as a result of paying such fees would not necessarily be the most efficient, nor the one with the best product offer; rather it would be the one best able to make the payment. The slotting fees would be acting as a barrier to entry to new suppliers.[112]

On the other hand, retailers may require slotting allowances in order to compensate them for the risks and costs associated with stocking a new, unproven product. Agreeing to stock a new product often means that another product must be dropped from the retailer's current stock. Under these circumstances, it may be reasonable for retailers to ask the manufacturer to bear some of the risk and costs involved in order to induce the retailer to stock the product, provided that the payment is proportionate to the risk-adjusted costs. However, where only a few retailers dominate the market, they are more likely to be able to require manufacturers to pay them, eg, slotting allowances. If there is limited competition between these few retailers, they will be more likely to retain the allowance as profit rather than passing it on to the consumer. The UK Competition Commission's report into supermarkets concluded that the practice of requiring slotting allowances and listing fees, when carried out by multiples with buyer power, adversely affects the competitiveness of some suppliers and distorts competition between suppliers. This is because 'the multiple engaging in the practice does not necessarily select the best, or most efficiently produced, product, or that preferred by customers, but to some extent is influenced by whoever is best able to make the payment requested.'[113]

[112] Competition Commission, *Supermarkets: a report on the supply of groceries from multiple stores in the United Kingdom, Vol 1: Summary and Conclusions* (London: The Stationery Office, 2000), 2.474.

[113] Idem, 2.476(c) and 2.477(c).

USA

Such practices will be subject to analysis under the Robinson–Patman Act where the payments are requested within the USA. The Federal Trade Commission (FTC) has been reluctant to condemn the practice in the absence of harm to consumers, and proposals for guidelines on slotting allowances in the grocery industry have met with some resistance.[114] The FTC recognises that the term 'slotting allowance' applies to a wide range of practices, 'the legality of which can be determined only in the light of all the surrounding facts and circumstances'.[115] Its approach involves evaluating a particular practice by determining what is to be offered in exchange for the payment from manufacturer to retailer. This will help to ascertain how much shelf-space is left for other suppliers, and consequently whether the allowances are detrimental or harmless, pro-competitive or anti-competitive.[116] The FTC will examine agreements between retailers and manufacturers that provide for slotting allowances or listing fees in light of the Robinson-Patman Act and the FTC's Fred Meyer Guidelines. The latter provide practical guidance on compliance with the Robinson–Patman Act and deal explicitly with slotting allowances.

Section 2(d) of the Robinson–Patman Act applies to a payment by a seller to a buyer of goods for services or facilities provided by the buyer in relation to the resale of the goods. This section provides that the allowances must be available to all buyers on proportionally equal terms. No single way of achieving this is prescribed by law; rather the Fred Meyer guidelines specify that any method that treats competing customers on proportionally equal terms may be used.[117] Furthermore, there must be a real *quid pro quo* for the allowance, such that the retailer must provide an actual service in order to justify the payment of the allowance. The guidelines warn that '[t]he discriminatory purchase of display or shelf-space, whether directly or by means of so-called allowances, may violate the Act, and may be considered an unfair method of competition in violation of the Federal Trade Commission Act.'[118] In other words, it must be determined whether a slotting allowance agreement is likely to result in manufacturers paying slotting allowances only to those retailers with sufficient buyer power to demand them. If so, the resulting competitive advantage enjoyed

114 See, eg, CJ MacAvoy, *Enforcement policy regarding slotting allowances*, paper presented at the Federal Trade Commission workshop on slotting allowances and other market practices, Washington, DC, 31 May–1 June 2000, p 7 ff., <*http://www.ftc.gov/bc/slotting/presentations/slottingallow.pdf*>.

115 'Slotting Allowances and the Antitrust Laws', Testimony of the FTC before the House Committee on the Judiciary, US House of Representatives, Washington, DC, 20 Oct, 1999.

116 Idem.

117 Federal Trade Commission: *Guides for Advertising Allowances and Other Merchandising Payments and Services*, 16 CFR §240.9.

118 Idem, §240.9, example 5 n 1.

by those retailers, in addition to market foreclosure at the supply level, are likely to be held to injure competition.

In *McCormick & Co*, the FTC investigated an alleged violation of the Robinson-Patman Act by a supplier of spices with a high market share. The supplier was allegedly charging some retailers a substantially higher price for its products than it charged other competing retailers, by providing competing retailers with discriminatory aggregate discounts off the list price of its products.[119] Here the discounts allegedly received by the retailers included up-front cash payments similar to slotting allowances, as well as rebates, free goods and performance funds. The FTC pursued its investigation into the firm by focusing on whether the company had agreements with retailers that gave it the ability to control retailer shelf-space and exclude competitors. This approach by the FTC highlights that investigations into slotting allowances will focus on the competitive advantages that slotting allowances offer to manufacturers. Therefore manufacturers will be prevented from agreeing to slotting allowance payments where these payments are likely to be agreed with only a small number of retailers on equally proportionate terms.

Manufacturers will not able to rely on the cost-justification defence, which is available to rebut a charge of price-discrimination under section 2(a) of the Act; however, the defence of meeting the competition may be available to rebut a case of unlawful discrimination. A manufacturer would have to demonstrate that the allowance provided to the retailer was offered in good faith in order to meet that of a competitor. Case-law stipulates that the manufacturer must verify the competitor's allowance as well as ensure that the discriminatory allowance to be offered will meet, but not beat, that of the competitor.[120] Otherwise this will amount to a discriminatory allowance and will violate the Robinson–Patman Act.

France

In France, at present, listing fees that do not confer any *quid pro quo* are prohibited. Article L. 442-6(I)(2) provides that retailers requesting a listing fee must commit to a minimum purchase proportionate to the listing fee, although the law is silent as to what would be proportionate. Further rules in Article L.420-2 prevent a retailer with a dominant position on the French market, or a retailer upon which suppliers are economically dependent, from abusively exploiting such a position. The requirement of listing fees may constitute an abuse, as discriminatory sales conditions are specifically mentioned in the provision. It should be noted that the New

119 *McCormick & Co.*, FTC File No. 961-0050. The Company agreed to comply with the FTC's Decision and Order of 27 Apr 2000, Docket No C-3939.

120 See *Standard Oil Co. v FTC*, 340 US 231 (1951); *FTC v A.E. Staley Mfg Co*, 324 US 746 (1959); See *Moss, Inc v FTC*, 148 F.2d 378 (2d Cir 1945).

Economic Relations Bill has introduced new rules to prohibit abusive listing fees, for example where they are paid without suppliers being guaranteed that their product will in fact be purchased. This would appear to constitute a more general prohibition in order to avoid the legal uncertainty raised by the previous requirement of proportionality.

United Kingdom

The practice of retailers requiring slotting allowances and listing fees from suppliers has come under scrutiny in the UK Competition Commission's report on supermarkets. As discussed above, the Competition Commission found that competition was distorted at the supply level when retailers with buyer power required payments or concessions in order to gain access to supermarkets' shelf-space and for better positioning of their products within the stores.[121] In addition, while the Office of Fair Trading has included slotting fees in examples of vertical restraints that are common business practice, it stipulates that slotting fees may foreclose markets at the supply level, because the fees may represent a sunk cost, and at the retail level, since they provide non-cost related discounts to existing retailers.[122]

On the basis of findings of adverse effects with regard to practices concerning suppliers and retailers, the Competition Commission recommended that any multiple with more than 8 per cent of grocery purchases for resale from its stores should be required to give undertakings to comply with a code of practice. The Commission specified that the code should include provisions that would prohibit payment to multiples as a condition for slotting or listing existing products or for better positioning of products within stores, or for increasing shelf-space allocated to particular products.[123] Limiting the provision to existing products is a recognition that retailers have a legitimate interest in reducing their exposure to the risks and costs involved in agreeing to stock a new product, by requiring that suppliers pay risk-adjusted costs. However this would apply only to qualifying retailers operating in the UK market in their relations with UK-based suppliers. The Code of Practice adopted binds the largest four supermarkets; paragraph 9 stipulates that listing fees are not to be charged except for new product lines, and in addition the fee must reflect 'the risk run by that supermarket in stocking, displaying or listing such new products'.[124]

[121] Competition Commission, *Supermarkets: a report on the supply of groceries from multiple stores in the United Kingdom, Vol 1: Summary and Conclusions* (London: The Stationery Office, 2000), 2.474–2.477.

[122] Office of Fair Trading: *Director General of Fair Trading's Guidelines: The Chapter II Prohibition*, OFT 402 (Mar 1999), paras 4.34 and 4.38, reprinted in G Lindrup (ed), *Butterworth's Competition Law Handbook*, 6th edn (London: Butterworths, 2000), p 356.

[123] Competition Commission, *Supermarkets: a report on the supply of groceries from multiple stores in the United Kingdom, Vol 1: Summary and Conclusions* (London: The Stationery Office, 2000), 2.588(j).

[124] See Annex.

Other promotional moneys

Retailers may require manufacturers to make payments in return for promotion of their products within the retailers' stores. Such payments may include promotional contributions, advertising support and promotional display support. The competition issues raised here mirror those identified in relation to requiring slotting allowances and listing fees. Consequently the payment of promotional moneys is in general regulated in the same manner. The purpose of this section is to highlight additional regulations in France and in the United Kingdom that are specific to promotional moneys.

France

In France, the New Economic Regulations Law clarifies the legal framework applicable to special offers. The current rules relate to pre-contractual transparency and impose strict invoicing requirements and sanctions for failing to comply with the provisions.[125]

United Kingdom

The UK Competition Commission's report on supermarkets investigated practices that required suppliers to make payments for, among other things, annual in-store promotions, specific advertising, and special promotional packaging. Competition between retailers is distorted because those retailers that do not receive the discounts are disadvantaged; and competition between suppliers is distorted because the retailer 'engaging in the practice does not necessarily select the best, or most efficiently produced, product, or that preferred by customers, but to some extent is influenced by whoever is best able to make the payment requested'.[126] The Competition Commission therefore recommended that the proposed code of practice should include a provision whereby retailers must give suppliers reasonable notice of any intention to hold a promotion in relation to the supplier's products where there is likely to be a significant impact on the supplier's costs; and they should not require suppliers to fund promotions to a predominant extent.[127] The implementation of the code, which incorporates these provisions in paragraphs 11–14, will affect agreements on promotional moneys between retailers operating in the UK and their UK-based suppliers.[128]

[125] Articles L. 441-3 and L. 441-4 of the Code de Commerce.

[126] Competition Commission, *Supermarkets: a report on the supply of groceries from multiple stores in the United Kingdom, Vol 1: Summary and Conclusions* (London: The Stationery Office, 2000), 2.476(c), 2.479 and 2.483.

[127] Ibid, 2.588(i).

[128] See Annex.

Abuse of economic dependency

It should be considered whether unified trading terms might contravene national legislation designed to tackle the abuse of economic dependence. The purpose of these provisions is to extend the reach of abuse of dominance laws to situations where buyers who are not dominant in their selling market are nevertheless in a position of strength in relation to other firms. A supplier would therefore be considered economically dependent if there were no equivalent alternative to a certain retailer as an outlet, or where the retailer is a supplier's only possible partner. The resulting imbalance between retailer and supplier leads to a disparity in their respective negotiation powers.[129] A retailer in this position would be able to obtain supply terms and conditions which would not be granted by a manufacturer under normal competitive conditions. The fact that these laws are an extension of abuse of dominance provisions means that it will not be sufficient for a supplier to show that it is dependent upon a retailer and that it has been harmed as a result. An anti-competitive effect on the market must be demonstrated.

Germany

The prohibition against the abuse of economic dependence in Germany has its roots in a policy of protecting small and medium-sized enterprises. Following the 6th amendment to the GWB, the prohibitions of discrimination and hindrance are found in Paragraph 20(1)–(3). Paragraph 20(1) provides that market-dominating enterprises, cartels exempted under Paragraphs 2 to 8 of the Act and enterprises instigating RPM within the exemptions in Paragraphs 15, 28(2), 29(2) and 30(1) of the GWB, are prohibited from unfairly hindering another undertaking, or according unjustified different treatment to similar enterprises. This prohibition is extended by Paragraph 20(2) to undertakings with vertical relative market power in relation to any small or medium-sized suppliers or purchasers that are dependent upon that firm because they have no reasonable alternative to shift their business to other firms. The second sentence of Paragraph 20(2) provides a presumption of such dependence where a purchaser regularly receives special benefits from the supplier which are not granted to similar purchasers. Paragraph 20(3) further prohibits a firm having such power from discriminating against or unreasonably restraining these small or medium-sized undertakings.

If a supplier is a 'small or medium-sized enterprise', and can demonstrate that it is economically dependent upon a particular retailer operating

[129] OECD, *Buying power of multiproduct retailers: background paper by the Secretariat* (Paris, 1999), p 41. See also European Commission decisions in retail merger cases, such as *Rewe/Meinl*, paras 98–106.

in the German market, or can provide evidence of benefits accorded to the retailer from which economic dependence will be presumed, and it suffers loss as a result of breach by the retailer of the legislative provisions referred to above, it can recover damages from, and/or obtain injunctive relief against the retailer under Paragraph 33 of the GWB, without having to wait for the Bundeskartellamt to take action. In addition, Paragraph 54 GWB allows those suppliers who wish to complain about the abuse of retailer buyer power to remain anonymous during the investigations by the BKA.

France

In France, an abuse of economic dependence provision is found in the broader provision prohibiting anti-competitive abuses of a dominant position in the Code de Commerce. Article L. 420-2(I)(2) prohibits an undertaking or group of undertakings from taking unfair advantage of a client or supplier business which is economically dependent upon it and which has no equivalent alternative, where the unfair advantage has the effect of distorting competition on a given market. However, there is no definition of what will constitute an 'equivalent alternative'. The provision lists refusal to supply, tied sales, discriminatory conditions of sale, and the breaking off of business relations on the sole ground that the other party refuses to submit to unjustified conditions of business, as examples of such abuse. Article L420-2(I)(2) is supplemented by the general prohibition on discriminatory sales and purchasing conditions contained in Article L. 442-6. This recognises the imbalance of bargaining power associated with a state of economic dependence and specifies cases that amount to dependence that no longer require proof that the abuse has a restrictive effect on the market as a whole. Obtaining or attempting to obtain an advantage as a precondition for issuing orders is prohibited by Article L. 442-6(I)(2), unless accompanied by a written commitment to make a proportionate volume of purchases. Article L. 442-6(I)(3) prohibits the threat of a sudden breaking-off of commercial relations in order to receive unjustified commercial advantages, while Article L. 442-6(I)(4) prohibits the sudden termination of an established commercial relationship without notice. These provisions do not require formal proof of economic dependence, which has been difficult to establish under L. 420-2(I)(2) for a particular description of goods.

5. CONCLUSION

The importance of retailing is clear: a lack of competition at the retail level has direct adverse effects for consumers. If the retail markets are concentrated enough, especially where retailers succeed in differentiating themselves using private label and other techniques, retailers may acquire sufficient power to be able unilaterally to raise prices or engage in other market distorting behaviour. Changes in the retail market require enhanced enforcement action. Competition authorities may therefore need to refine market definitions in cases involving large-scale retailers. Also there is an argument for rethinking parts of competition policy, especially with regard to vertical restraints. For example, the arguments favouring *per se* prohibitions of RPM should be reconsidered in the context that retailers are now both competitors and customers of their suppliers. Competition authorities ought to go beyond the strict application of antitrust tools to increasingly concentrated and segmented retail markets, and should advocate the repeal of laws and legislative proposals offering dubious protection to smaller manufacturers and retailers. For example the protection afforded to manufacturers through loss-leading provisions is doubtful and may instead reduce price competition beneficial to consumers.[130]

It is often argued that competition authorities face a possible trade-off in cases involving buyer power. They will face pressure from those that argue that competition requires competitors and that they are equally deserving of protection from unfair bargaining power. However, this should be accompanied by an important caveat: protecting competition will protect competitors also, but only those which are efficient in meeting consumers' needs.[131]

130 OECD, *Buying power of multi-product retailers*, Background paper by the Secretariat (Paris, 1999), p 46.

131 Idem.

ANNEX

Code of Practice on Supermarkets' Dealings with Suppliers[132]

HAVING REGARD TO the Fair Trading Act 1973;

HAVING REGARD TO the Supermarkets Report of the Competition Commission;

RECOGNISING that:
(a) a competitive market is the most effective way of protecting the interests of UK consumers;
(b) in a free and fair market place, the Supermarkets compete with each other in the level of service, quality of product and value for money that they offer to UK consumers; and
(c) it is in the interests of UK consumers that Supermarkets should constantly seek to improve their operating efficiency.

WHEREAS:
(a) The Competition Commission has recommended that a code of practice should be introduced to put relations between Supermarkets and their Suppliers on a clearer and more predictable basis.
(b) The Competition Commission found that the undue exercise of buyer power by Supermarkets in the circumstances identified in the Supermarkets Report has effects which are against the public interest.
(c) The Director, following consultation with the Supermarkets, has devised this Code of practice to meet the concerns of the Competition Commission without wishing to inhibit mutually beneficial arrangements genuinely entered into by Supermarkets and their Suppliers.
(d) The effective operation of this Code depends upon both the Supermarkets and their Suppliers being reasonable in their dealings with each other.
(e) The Director expects that the dispute resolution procedure provided for in this Code will be effective and that mediation is the most appropriate way of resolving disputes arising under the Code.
(f) The Supermarkets are fully committed to the objectives of this Code and undertake to operate under this Code in good faith.

NOW THEREFORE this Code has effect:

PART 1—STANDARD TERMS OF BUSINESS

Terms of business to be available in writing

1 The terms of business offered by a Supermarket for its dealings with a Supplier shall be available in writing at the request of that Supplier such that:

[132] See DTI press release P/2001/606 of 31 Oct 2001.

(a) the standard terms of business offered to all Suppliers, or to all Suppliers in a particular category, shall be available at the request of any Supplier in that category; and
(b) the particular terms of business offered to any one Supplier shall be available at the request of that Supplier.

2 Reasonable Notice of variation of a Supermarket's terms of business shall be given to the affected Supplier(s).

No undue delay in Payments

3 A Supermarket shall pay a Supplier for products delivered to that Supermarket's specification within a reasonable time after the date of that Supplier's invoice.

PART 2—PRICES & PAYMENTS

No retrospective reduction in price without Reasonable Notice

4 A Supermarket shall not directly or indirectly require a Supplier to reduce the agreed price of or increase the agreed discount for any product unless Reasonable Notice of such requirement is given to that Supplier in writing before the relevant supplies of that product are made.

No obligation to contribute to marketing costs

5 A Supermarket shall not, directly or indirectly, Unreasonably Require a Supplier to make any Payment towards that Supermarket's costs of:
(a) buyer visits to new or prospective Suppliers;
(b) artwork or packaging design;
(c) consumer or market research;
(d) the opening or refurbishing of a store; or
(e) hospitality for that Supermarket's staff.

No Payments for lower profits unless the basis of Payment is agreed in advance

6 A Supermarket shall not directly or indirectly require a Supplier to make any Payment to compensate that Supermarket when profits from the sale of that Supplier's products are lower than expected by that Supermarket unless the basis of any such Payment is agreed in writing between that Supermarket and that Supplier before the relevant supplies of that product are made.

No Payments for wastage without prior agreement, negligence or default

7 A Supermarket shall not directly or indirectly require a Supplier to

make any Payment to cover any wastage of that Supplier's products incurred at that Supermarket's stores unless:

(a) such wastage is due to the negligence or default of that Supplier; or

(b) the basis of such Payment is agreed in writing between that Supermarket and that Supplier before the relevant supplies of that product are made.

8 A Supermarket shall use its best endeavours to agree in writing with a Supplier what principal factors in their dealings would be likely to amount to negligence or default on the part of that Supplier.

Limited circumstances for lump sum payments as a condition of being a Supplier

9 Supermarket shall not directly or indirectly require a Supplier to make any lump sum payment as a condition of stocking or listing that Supplier's products unless either:

(a) such payment is made in relation to a Promotion; or

(b) such payment:

(i) is made in respect of new products which have not been stocked, displayed or listed by that Supermarket during the preceding 365 days in 25pct or more of its stores; and

(ii) reflects a reasonable estimate by that Supermarket of the risk run by that Supermarket in stocking, displaying or listing such new products.

No lump sum payments for better positioning of goods unless in relation to Promotions

10 A Supermarket shall not directly or indirectly require a Supplier to make any lump sum payment in order to secure better positioning or an increase in the allocation of shelf space for any products of that Supplier within a store unless such payment is made in relation to a Promotion.

PART 3—PROMOTIONS

No Promotions without Reasonable Notice

11 Where a Supermarket directly or indirectly requires any Payment from a Supplier in support of a Promotion of one of that Supplier's products, a Supermarket shall only hold that Promotion after Reasonable Notice has been given to that Supplier in writing.

Due care to be taken when ordering for Promotions

12 A Supermarket shall take due care when ordering products from a

Supplier at a promotional wholesale price not to over-order, and, if that Supermarket fails to take such care, it shall compensate that Supplier for any product over-ordered and which it subsequently sells at a higher non-promotional retail price.

13 A Supermarket shall ensure that the basis on which any order for a Promotion is calculated is transparent.

Suppliers not predominantly to fund Promotions

14 A Supermarket shall not, directly or indirectly, Unreasonably Require a Supplier predominantly to fund the costs of a Promotion.

PART 4—COMPENSATION

No change to supply chain procedures without Reasonable Notice or compensation

15 A Supermarket shall not directly or indirectly require a Supplier to change significantly any aspect of the normal supply chain procedures unless that Supermarket either:

(a) gives Reasonable Notice of such change to that Supplier in writing; or

(b) fully compensates that Supplier for any net resulting costs incurred as a direct result of the failure to give Reasonable Notice.

No change to specifications without Reasonable Notice or compensation

16 A Supermarket shall not directly or indirectly require a Supplier to change the specification (including the quantity of products required) of any agreed order unless that Supermarket either:

(a) gives Reasonable Notice of such change to that Supplier in writing; or

(b) fully compensates that Supplier for any net resulting costs incurred as a direct result of the failure to give Reasonable Notice.

Limited circumstances for compensation for erroneous forecasts

17 Notwithstanding clauses [15] and [16] above, a Supermarket shall fully compensate a Supplier for any cost incurred by that Supplier as a result of any forecasting error attributable to that Supermarket unless:

(a) that Supermarket has prepared those forecasts in good faith and with due care; or

(b) there is an agreement in writing between that Supermarket and that Supplier before the relevant supplies of the product are made that such compensation is not appropriate.

18 A Supermarket shall ensure that the basis on which it prepares any forecast is transparent.

PART 5—CONSUMER COMPLAINTS

No unjustified Payment for consumer complaints

19 Subject to clause [21] below, where any consumer complaint can be resolved in store by a Supermarket refunding the retail price or replacing the relevant product, that Supermarket shall not directly or indirectly require a Supplier to make any Payment for resolving such a complaint unless:

(a) the Payment does not exceed the retail price of the product charged by that Supermarket;

(b) that Supermarket is satisfied on reasonable grounds that the consumer complaint is justifiable and attributable to a failing on the part of that Supplier; and

(c) that Supermarket gives notice to that Supplier of such complaint.

20 Subject to clause [21] below, where any consumer complaint cannot be resolved in store by a Supermarket refunding the retail price or replacing the relevant product, that Supermarket shall not directly or indirectly require a Supplier to make any Payment for resolving such a complaint unless:

(a) the Payment is reasonably related to that Supermarket's costs arising from that complaint;

(b) that Supermarket has verified that the consumer complaint is justifiable and attributable to a failing on the part of that Supplier; and

(c) a full report about the complaint (including the basis of the attribution) has been made by that Supermarket to that Supplier.

21 A Supermarket may agree with a Supplier an average figure for Payments for resolving such complaints as an alternative to accounting for complaints individually.

PART 6—THIRD PARTY DEALINGS

No tying third party goods and services for Payment

22 A Supermarket shall not directly or indirectly require a Supplier to obtain any goods, services or property from any third party where that Supermarket obtains any Payment for this arrangement from any third party, unless the Supplier's alternative source for those goods, services or property:

(a) fails to meet the objective quality standards laid down for that Supplier by that Supermarket for the supply of such goods, services or property; or

(b) charges more than any other third party recommended by that Supermarket for the supply of such goods, services or property.

PART 7—STAFF TRAINING

Obligatory training for buyers

23 A Supermarket shall supply a copy of this Code to all Grocery buying staff.

24 A Supermarket shall provide training on the requirements of this Code to all Grocery buying staff.

25 A Supermarket shall furnish to the Director an annual return detailing staff training and guidance issued in relation to this Code in such form and on such days as the Director may specify from time to time.

PART 8—GENERAL

Compliance and Dispute Resolution

26 A Supermarket shall negotiate in good faith with a Supplier to resolve any dispute arising under the terms of this Code.

27 If bi-lateral negotiations under clause [26] above cannot resolve a dispute within 90 days of that dispute arising, a Supermarket shall at its own expense offer the services of the Mediator to assist.

28 If the Mediator under clause [27] above has failed to resolve a dispute, the Supermarket shall give notice to the Director.

29 A Supermarket shall notify the contact details of any Mediator to the Director.

30 A Supermarket shall procure the Mediator to supply to the Director:

(a) an annual return of its work under this Code in such form and on such days as the Director may specify from time to time; and

(b) such other information as the Director may specify from time to time in relation to individual cases on which the Director is considering taking action.

Interpretation

31 For the avoidance of doubt, compliance with this Code does not affect the duty on any person to comply with or restrict the application of the Competition Act 1998.

32 In this Code:

'the Director' means the Director General of Fair Trading;

'Groceries' are products sold from any retail store in the United Kingdom and include food, pet food, alcoholic and non alcoholic drinks, cleaning products, toiletries (dental care products, soap, hair care, sanitary protection, nappies and similar products) and household goods (tissues, kitchen rolls, food wraps, bin liners, light bulbs and similar products) but exclude food and alcoholic and non alcoholic drinks sold for consumption in the store where it is purchased, petrol, clothing, DIY products, financial services, pharmaceuticals, newspapers, magazines, greetings cards, compact discs, video and audio tapes, toys, plants, flowers, perfumes, cosmetics, electrical appliances, kitchen hardware, gardening equipment, books, tobacco and tobacco products and Grocery means any one of them;

'Group of Interconnected Bodies Corporate' has the meaning given in section 137(5) of the Fair Trading Act 1973;

'the Mediator' means such independent person or persons as shall be appointed by a Supermarket under clause [27] above from time to time to provide mediation services;

'Payment' or 'Payments' includes an inducement in any form (monetary or otherwise) and includes better contractual terms;

'Person' includes a body of persons corporate or unincorporate;

'Promotion' means any offer for sale at an introductory or a reduced retail price, or with some additional benefit to consumers that is intended to be only for a specified period;

the meaning of 'Reasonable Notice' in clauses [2, 4, 11, 15 or 16] depends on the circumstances of each case including, for example:

(a) whether the notice period given is objectively justifiable and this depends on the circumstances of each case including, for example:
  (i) the duration of any relevant contract or the frequency with which orders are placed by the Supermarket for relevant Groceries;
  (ii) the characteristics of the relevant Groceries and their production including durability and dependency on external factors such as the weather;
  (iii) the value of any relevant order relative to the turnover of the Supplier in question; and
  (iv) the overall impact on the business of the Supplier of the information given in the notice;

(b) whether the reasons for the notice period given are transparent; and

(c) whether similar cases are treated alike;

'the Supermarkets Report' means the report of the Competition Commission on the supply of Groceries from multiple stores in the United Kingdom presented to Parliament in October 2000 (Cm 4842);

'Supermarkets' means all retailers of Groceries with 8pct or more of the market for the purchase of Groceries for resale from their stores in the United Kingdom and 'Supermarket' means any one of them;

'Supplier' means any Person actually or potentially carrying on a business in the supply of Groceries to any Supermarket, such Person being established anywhere in the world but, in relation to any Supermarket, excludes any Person which is a member of the same Group of Interconnected Bodies Corporate as that Supermarket; and

'Unreasonably Require' in clauses [5] and [14] excludes a case where a Supplier genuinely volunteers to make a Payment in response to ordinary commercial pressures, provided that, where those pressures are partly or wholly attributable to a Supermarket, they shall only be deemed to be ordinary commercial pressures where they are objectively justifiable, transparent and result in similar cases being treated alike.